NARCOS

THE ART AND MAKING OF THE SHOW

NARCOS
THE ART AND MAKING OF THE SHOW

ISBN: 9781785659089

Published by Titan Books
A division of Titan Publishing Group Ltd.
144 Southwark St.
London
SE1 0UP

First edition: November 2018
10 9 8 7 6 5 4 3 2 1

Did you enjoy this book? We love to hear from our readers.
Please e-mail us at: readerfeedback@titanemail.com or write to Reader Feedback at the above address.

To receive advance information, news, competitions, and exclusive offers online, please sign up for the Titan newsletter on our website: www.titanbooks.com

A CIP catalogue record for this title is available from the British Library.

Printed and bound in China.

NARCOS

THE ART AND MAKING OF THE SHOW

WRITTEN BY JEFF BOND

FOREWORD BY ERIC NEWMAN, DOUG MIRO, AND CARLO BERNARD

TITAN BOOKS

CONTENTS

CALI CARTEL

GUADALAJARA CARTEL

ACKNOWLEDGEMENTS

FOREWORD

By Eric Newman, Doug Miro, and Carlo Bernard

Though many disagree on how and why, it seems a unanimous opinion that we are losing the war on drugs. Though we sought to look closely at what has quietly become America's longest running and costliest undeclared war, we never took it upon ourselves to offer a conclusive analysis one way or another. We couldn't do that even if we had wanted to as the tragedy of this conflict is outweighed only by its complexity. Sixty years of politics, money, colonialism, arrogance, ignorance, imperialism, violence, addiction, and horrible policy: all of these concepts combining with the most powerful stimulant ever created to form a free-base cocktail of lethal potency and a body count well into the millions. Yeah, tackling that was never our objective. We were instead drawn to the people, and personalities, on both sides of the drug war. It was our goal to depict them like they really were, and while

much of what they did seems too strange to believe, one of the great strengths of Narcos is that the stories we tell are almost always the truth—particularly the really crazy shit. An article we read somewhere referred to us as "pulp non-fiction." That sounds about right. The pulp is sometimes the truest thing we do. But the non-fiction is what really blows you away. Authenticity is everything for us. And the crew we put to together in Colombia and now in Mexico brought a reality to our storytelling that can't be praised enough. The production design, costumes, locations share center stage with our actors and our story. We are proud of our directors and crew, almost entirely Latin American, and are grateful to Gaumont and Netflix for letting us make this show in the place where it happened: the only place where the story could be told.

ABOVE: Director José Padilha (far left), Eric Newman (center), Chris Brancato (far right) and crew during the filming of the episode 'The Sword of Simón Bolivar.'

INTRODUCTION

Creating a Historical Drama

Narcos premiered on Netflix as an immediate, global hit for the streaming network, as well as for the creators of the show, and for its studio Gaumont. The show generated a worldwide fan base and critical acclaim—and it did so by breaking some of the most hallowed rules of Hollywood production. This is the story of how *Narcos* came to be, and how the incredible talents both in front of and behind the camera contributed to its success.

The series became a hit by telling, with vivid detail and authenticity, a historical saga so staggering in its violence, scope, and impact that viewers going in would have to assume that most of the show's most memorable moments were highly fictionalized. But the real shock came when news footage from the actual era showed audiences that these events really happened, often exactly the way they are represented on the show. The show's fidelity to the history of the Colombian drug cartels and the cocaine trade was so authentic that Netflix promoted the show with narcopedia: a site providing additional historical context to the show's characters and situations.

J.L.Fisher

LEFT: Behind the camera on 'The Good, The Bad, and the Dead' with director Andrés Baiz.
ABOVE: Pablo has a private conversation with his most trusted partner, Gustavo.

The first bilingual series of its kind, *Narcos* is jokingly referred to in Latin America as "the show that finally made *gringos* read subtitles." It features a primarily Latin American cast and is helmed mostly by Latin American directors. The show is shot on location in Colombia, sometimes exactly where the actual events depicted on the series took place—transporting American viewers to a world most have never before experienced. The result is an immersive experience that has turned *Narcos* into a hit series, quoted and referenced in other media, with a massive online fan following that generates imaginative artwork, theories, and analysis of its own.

Narcos launched its first season with one of the most legendary and notorious criminal figures in history. Pablo Escobar was the leader of the Medellín drug cartel and a man whose rise to power embraced smuggling, murder, politics, state corruption, and activities that required a new term to describe them: narco terrorism. The *Narcos* story, however, was even larger than Escobar, and would grow to encompass other drug cartels active in South America, the United States, and Mexico.

When creator and executive producer Eric Newman began the project in 1995 he originally planned to make a feature length film of the Pablo Escobar story. "I didn't know that much about

the drug war," says Newman. "I knew that we were never simply the good guys and that things were much more complicated." Newman's perspective about the shades of gray inherent in the story—which had been addressed in more black and white terms in other films and TV shows, with Colombian drug dealers shown as faceless monsters—would ultimately inform the show's nuanced and complex depiction of the drug trade, with heroes and villains on all sides.

The story of the hunt for Escobar involved a sprawling cast of real-life characters and spanned fifteen years, with numerous figures moving in and out of the narrative, and Newman soon decided that any attempt to depict Escobar in a movie was doomed, "In two hours Pablo can only be a bad guy—you can't take a guy who blows up an airliner at the beginning of the movie and redeem him in two hours, you just don't have time." The showrunner became convinced that the Escobar saga could be best addressed in long form television, where this incredible character, his associates and adversaries could be fleshed out as living, breathing human beings.

"In 2012 I got into business with Netflix with the series *Hemlock Grove*," Eric Newman says, "and Gaumont had come in as the studio, and I learned that they were looking to expand into

South America, and they asked me if I had anything that could work with them in that space." He began discussing the idea of a Pablo Escobar project with José Padilha, who had a background in documentaries—his *Elite Squad* movies were fact-based thrillers about a military police force taking down drug dealers in Brazil. "I said I could repurpose the drug war project as a television show, and since I was working with José Padilha I told them I even have a South American director. And I think Netflix was more excited about working on a José Padilha project than they were about doing a drug war show."

The project would eventually involve Eric Newman, José Padilha, Andrés Baiz, Chris Brancato, Doug Miro, and Carlo Bernard, all of whom would help hone the concept into what would become a large-scale production filmed on location in Colombia. Newman's original idea for the series was to focus the first two seasons of the show on the Medellín cartel, killing Escobar at the end of season two. His plan then included two years on Escobar's successors, the Cali cartel, followed by a year of the North Valley cartel and then a focus on Mexico, where the majority of cocaine that came into America would ultimately originate.

Screenwriters Doug Miro and Carlo Bernard were originally recruited to write the story from the perspective of U.S. Marine colonel Gil Macklin, who had helped train Colombian troops in the hunt for Escobar. It soon became clear that Macklin hadn't been in Colombia during many of the key events in the Escobar saga. But he knew two people who had: American DEA agents Steve Murphy and Javier Peña. Focusing on the DEA added complexity to the concept. "The challenge was getting at the gist of what the DEA does," Miro says. "The DEA is in other countries enforcing our drug laws, so that's an odd dynamic for these guys. They have to form these partnerships with local police who are often corrupt or have their own agendas or justifiably don't want to help some out-of-town *gringos* to do their jobs."

Murphy and Peña would be streetwise, emotionally vulnerable and sometimes morally compromised cops instead of stiff military personnel, a decision that would add immeasurably to the show's depth and unpredictability. "DEA agents are different," Miro says. "They want guys who can work informants, and working informants is its own art form. They're good talkers, they see angles, they don't take any bullshit." Miro and Bernard dove into research, visiting the DEA in Washington, the American ambassador who was in Colombia at the time, and Murphy and Peña themselves. "They knew every player in Colombia, all the stories, all of which is in the show," Miro adds.

Including archival footage to reinforce the factual events in the story was a crucial creative decision. Writer and executive producer Chris Brancato credits José Padilha, who also employed the technique in his *Elite Squad* movies. "José started

as a wonderful documentary filmmaker," Brancato says. "So when we were discussing the show he said we should put in documentary footage." The creative team then hired a separate editor, Luis Carballar, to gather a variety of archival footage—a difficult job considering it was set in 1980s Colombia. "We managed to find some great pieces," says Brancato, "including some campaign commercials for [Colombian president] César Gaviria, and I think audiences appreciated that."

Another element that raised the level of authenticity on the show and emerged organically out of the early meetings with Netflix was to have the narco characters speak in their native language. Recalling how he fixated on the idea of breaking the language barrier, Eric Newman remembered watching obscure war movies on LA's Z Channel as a teenager: "I always disliked the ones where the Germans spoke English with an accent." The scripts were written in English and translated into Spanish, which meant that native speakers, especially Colombians, like Andrés Baiz (who became a producer/director and co-executive producer of the series in season two) were instrumental in preserving authenticity. "When the script was ready, I then added Colombian authenticity to the pages: the way we speak, behavior in characters, cultural idiosyncrasies," Baiz explains. "Although most of the directors on the show are Latin-American, I'm the only Colombian director." One of Baiz's many responsibilities was to try and balance the heroic elements of the DEA, so the Colombian authorities were portrayed in an honest, truthful light. "We didn't want audiences to see the DEA as the white saviors of Colombia, rescuing damsels in distress. Both the heroic deeds and unethical behavior of both American and Colombian forces needed to be represented fairly."

Narcos seasons one and two told the story of Pablo Escobar in sometimes epic, often intimate detail—a real-life, historical train wreck that viewers couldn't look away from. Wagner Moura's performance as Escobar held audiences and critics so spellbound that many left the second season finale wondering how the show could possibly equal the psychodrama of Escobar's saga. The answer lay in one of the most incredible true stories of the Cali cartel. For the focus of season three, *Narcos* showrunner Eric Newman, working with Bernard and Miro, found a key inspiration in the story of an informant, Jorge Salcedo, trapped within the Cali cartel. Miro says, "We had done this rise and fall story with Pablo and this great story with this character who's both empathetic and monstrous, and now we had this totally different genre for season three because it was a thriller. It's about a guy who's trapped in a situation way beyond his control and how does he get out of it."

In later seasons, *Narcos* moves from South America to Mexico, ever nearer the locus of demand for cocaine in North America and the United States.

"THEY KNEW EVERY PLAYER IN COLOMBIA, ALL THE STORIES, ALL OF WHICH IS IN THE SHOW"

DOUG MIRO

ABOVE: Steve Murphy and Javier Peña were unlikely partners in the beginning.

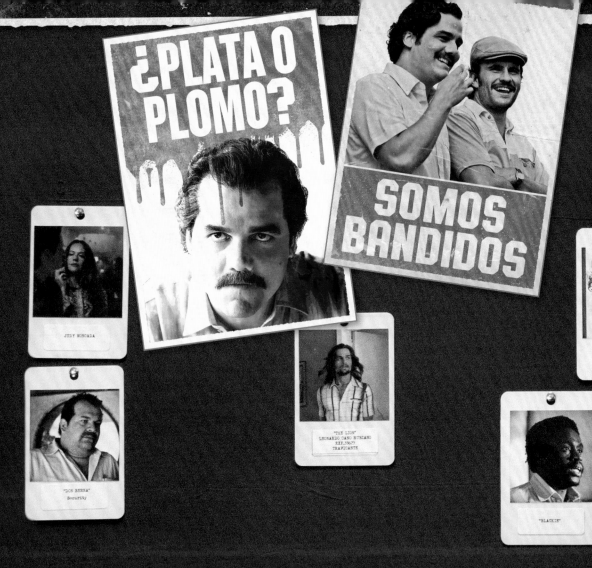

¿PLATA O PLOMO?

SOMOS BANDIDOS

PABLO

JUDY MONCADA

"LA QUICA"

"THE LION"
LEONARDO CANO RUBIANO
EXP.3567?
TRAFICANTE

"DON BERNA"
Security

"BLACKIE"

"LIM
CONDUCTOR

KEY LIEUTENANT
GERARDO MONCADA
"KIKO"
exp.16967
Medellin Cartel

GUSTAVO GAVIRIA

Sicario "SURE SHOT"
JUAN CORRALES
exp.9567
Medellin, Cartel

Sicario "POISON"
ROBERTO RAMOS
exp.1986
Medellin, Cartel

"Velasco"
RAUL VELASCO

Sicario "JAIRO"
exp.62579
Military trained,
Medellin Cartel

FERNANDO GALEANO

CAPO
MANUEL RODRIGUEZ GACHA
"EL MEXICANO"
exp.16896979
Medellin Cartel

Sicario "WOLFMAN"
JUAN CARLOS
exp.7436
Medellin, Cartel

Sicario "LAGARTO"
MARIO SALCEDO
exp.3579
Medellin, Cartel

Sicario "GORILLA"
BODYGUARD
exp.066252
Military trained,
Medellin Cartel

Sicario "SUGAR"
ALFONSO SAMSON
exp.736398
Medellin, Cart

MEDELLÍN

RICARDO FRISCO
EXP.232435
GUERRILLA
BANDA "LOS FRISCOS"

ROJAS
FINANZAS

CAPO
JORGE LUIS OCHOA V.
exp.364225
Medellín, Cartel

Sicario "MUGRE"
Military trained,
Medellín, Cartel

ACCOUNTANT
"BARBA NEGRA"
exp.0029629
Medellín Cartel

CAPO "FABIO OCHA"
KIDS ILICIT
BUSINESS ACTIVITY
exp.880429867
Medellín Cartel

EDGAR FRISCO
SICARIO
BANDA "LOS FRISCOS"

SICARIO "MORTERO"
EXP. 27876
ENTRENAMIENTO MILITAR

EDUARDO FRISCO
SICARIO
BANDA "LOS FRISCOS"

Sicario "ARETE"
Carlos Mario Alzate
exp.2003629
Military trained,
Medellín, Cartel

CAPO.
CARLOS LEHDER
exp.405657
Medellín, Cartel

Sicario "EL MENSAJE"
JOSE LUIS VALDES
exp.4527
Medellín, Cartel

Sicario "EL RONCA"
JHON MOLINA
exp.3455
Medellín, Cartel

Sicario "Cara Sucia"
exp.00950
Military trained,
Medellín, Cartel

Sicario "Big Mouth"
Julio Jimenez
exp.6276
Medellín, Cartel

In season one Eric Newman and Chris Brancato worked to condense fifteen years of Escobar's history into ten episodes.

"What I did with the writing staff was I looked at the span of his career," says Brancato. "So, from the beginning I wanted to have a tent pole idea for each of the ten episodes and then write the episode around whatever that tent pole was." The creative team then took a major event and made it the centerpiece of each episode: in the first one, Murphy and Escobar square off; the second one was the formation of the Medellín cartel because of the kidnapping of Marta Ochoa; in the third episode Pablo ran for congress. When he was booted out, it created an enormous resentment against the upper classes that was expressed in episode four when he blew up the Palace of Justice; in episode five Gaviria was elected; in episode six Gacha was killed; in episode seven Escobar started to kidnap the children of the upper classes; in episode eight he arranged his surrender deal which they called the "Big Lie" because he wasn't really surrendering; in episode nine he killed Moncada and Galeano in prison and in episode ten there was a raid on that prison and he escaped.

For the story of Escobar's flight, his descent from power, and eventual death in season two, Eric Newman, Doug Miro, and Carlo Bernard took advantage of the elaborate setup of season one that had established the Medellín cartel and its existence alongside the politics and culture of Colombia in such detail. "The idea in developing in our time with José and Eric was to try to really create a complex and vivid backdrop, so the show could be as much about the politics at work and not just a sort of cop show; not just a police procedural of trying to find Escobar," Bernard says. The writers were determined to take a global view of the story, with the background of the Cold War, economic considerations, and geopolitics all playing a part. America's position as a marketplace, and buyer of cocaine, and the source of money flowing into the trade added to the story's complexity. "We knew we wanted to be able to integrate in the stories both on a very human, micro level, a story about a family, whether it was Escobar's family or someone else's," explains Bernard. The creators also wanted to talk about how America engages with the rest of the world and how Colombia's own complex history was part of the narrative.

Ultimately the driver of the show's gripping drama in its first two seasons would still be the unforgettable figure of Pablo Escobar, a man who bullies and threatens his way to the heights of geopolitical power. "It's a deeply human story and, undeniably, he destroyed thousands of lives and certainly had it coming," Bernard says. "But at the same time to be able to also see him in human terms hopefully illustrates how tragic it is. To us, trying to dramatize the humanity of it hopefully makes it more tragic and not romanticizing him, but making him relatable, you're forced to reconcile the bad things this guy did, because you're forced to see him as a human being."

"IT'S A DEEPLY HUMAN STORY AND, UNDENIABLY, HE DESTROYED THOUSANDS OF LIVES"

CARLO BERNARD

TOP RIGHT: The Medellín cartel talks business.
BOTTOM RIGHT: Murphy and Peña on the hunt in the Medellín jungle.

PROFILE:
STEVE MURPHY

Based on a real-life DEA agent sent to Colombia, where he was partnered with agent Javier Peña, Steve Murphy functioned as an early way into *Narcos'* elaborate narrative. An English-speaking American with a basic understanding of the cocaine trade in the U.S., Steve filled the viewer in on background in Colombia as he himself learned the ropes of working in this foreign country. He's a man who found his moral compass gradually tested as he became personally invested in the hunt for Escobar.

Murphy arrived in Colombia as a fish out of water and was dependent on his new partner, Peña, to educate him on Colombian society and culture, the details of the drug trade and its dangerous narcos, and the ins and outs of the country's military and police forces that are often riddled with corruption. Murphy and his wife Connie (Joanna Christie) got a rude introduction to that aspect of their new life when they were held up at customs while entering the country.

Although the show aimed for a realistic portrayal of Colombia, the creators still wanted it to be appealing to people in the U.S. Using the character of Murphy to lead the viewers down to Colombia worked in bringing the American and Colombian sides of the drug war together in the first episode. While the creative team wanted to use Steve as an introduction to the story, they didn't want any suggestion that Americans

were "white hat heroes" that arrived in Colombia and saved the day. "In point of fact the Colombians were really the ones responsible for catching Escobar and killing him, and the American role was more supportive than lead," says Brancato.

Steve Murphy also played a major role as narrator of the first two seasons. It was José Padilha's involvement, and his experience on the *Elite Squad* movies, that brought this strategy to condense the wealth of information involving the drug war into a meaningful stream for viewers. "José was interested in me writing a lot of voiceover," Brancato says, "which at first really terrified me because voiceover can often be a cheat and make for not great drama, but after

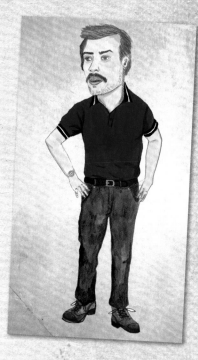

RIGHT: Costume sketch created by cosume designer María Estela Fernández.

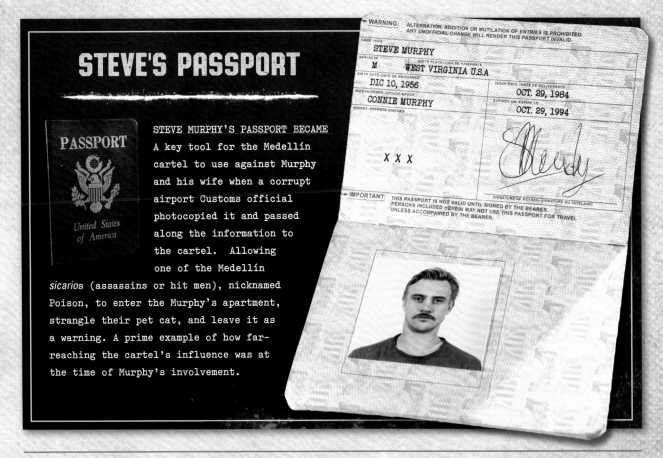

STEVE'S PASSPORT

STEVE MURPHY'S PASSPORT BECAME
A key tool for the Medellín cartel to use against Murphy and his wife when a corrupt airport Customs official photocopied it and passed along the information to the cartel. Allowing one of the Medellín *sicario*s (assassins or hit men), nicknamed Poison, to enter the Murphy's apartment, strangle their pet cat, and leave it as a warning. A prime example of how far-reaching the cartel's influence was at the time of Murphy's involvement.

WARNING: ALTERNATION, ADDITION OR MUTILATION OF ENTRIES IS PROHIBITED. ANY UNOFFICIAL CHANGE WILL RENDER THIS PASSPORT INVALID.

NAME-NOM STEVE MURPHY
SEX-SEXE M BIRTH PLACE-LIEU DE NAISSANCE WEST VIRGINIA U.S.A
BIRTH DATE-DATE DE NAISSANCE DIC 10, 1956
WIFE-HUSBAND-EPOUSE-EPOUX CONNIE MURPHY
MINORS-ENFANTS MINEURS

ISSUE DATE-DATE DE DELIVERANCE OCT. 29, 1984
EXPIRES ON-EXPIRE LE OCT. 29, 1994

X X X

IMPORTANT: THIS PASSPORT IS NOT VALID UNTIL SIGNED BY THE BEARER. PERSONS INCLUDED HEREIN MAY NOT USE THIS PASSPORT FOR TRAVEL UNLESS ACCOMPANIED BY THE BEARER.

THIS PAGE: DEA agent Steve Murphy in action.

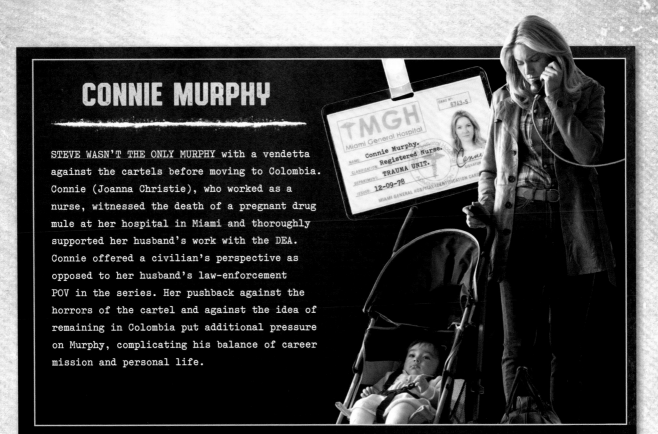

CONNIE MURPHY

STEVE WASN'T THE ONLY MURPHY with a vendetta against the cartels before moving to Colombia. Connie (Joanna Christie), who worked as a nurse, witnessed the death of a pregnant drug mule at her hospital in Miami and thoroughly supported her husband's work with the DEA. Connie offered a civilian's perspective as opposed to her husband's law-enforcement POV in the series. Her pushback against the horrors of the cartel and against the idea of remaining in Colombia put additional pressure on Murphy, complicating his balance of career mission and personal life.

"HE CAME TO COLOMBIA WITH SOME SORT OF NAÏVE IDEA HE CAN CHANGE THINGS"

ANDRÉS BAIZ

he suggested that I thought about two things. First, his *Elite Squad* movies are chockablock with voiceover, so I thought, 'oh, he wants to do a TV series that mirrors *Elite Squad*, that's a hell of a good idea actually.' I also read a blog about *Goodfellas* that said when the subject matter is so rich and detailed and journalistic, then voiceover is very helpful because you can point out little details and things that you can't afford to have in dialogue within the piece."

Casting the real-life characters proved challenging, but Boyd Holbrook (*Gone Girl, Logan*) was a perfect match for Murphy. "Boyd was not particularly well known at the time," Brancato says, "but he'd done some small movies, and not only was he excellent in those movies but he was from Kentucky, and Steve Murphy's from West Virginia, and they look similar and there was a realistic commonality between Boyd and Steve."

Over the course of two seasons, Steve Murphy moved from idealism to world-weary cynicism, taking out his frustrations on both American and Colombian citizens as the hunt for Escobar took its toll on the DEA agent physically and psychologically. "He came to Colombia with some sort of naïve idea he can change things and make a difference," director Andrés Baiz says. "Then slowly the foreign culture around him, and his obsession with capturing Escobar takes a toll on him, on his psyche and personality, and he gets darker, angrier, and starts putting his family aside. The actors playing the DEA agents were in tune with that—they welcomed that inequity. When the actors got a chance to explore that other side they were very motivated—they needed and wanted that immoral complexity in their characters, as much as the actors playing narcos needed humanity in theirs."

PROFILE:
JAVIER PEÑA

Javier Peña preceded Steve Murphy on assignment in Colombia and had a greater comfort level with the systemic corruption in the country than Murphy, often sleeping with prostitutes to gain information on local criminals. After the death of Pablo Escobar, Peña continued working with the Colombian police's Search Bloc unit as well as the CIA and DEA to help bring down the Cali cartel members.

When looking to cast Peña, actor Pedro Pascal (*Game of Thrones, Kingsman: The Golden Circle*) ended up landing the role—but not right away. "Carmen Cuba, our casting director for some of the major roles, showed us Pedro on the very first day we started casting," Brancato says. "A lot of times you see actors on that first day and they're at a horrible disadvantage because you can't compare them to anybody else and you're not sure exactly what you want. So, we watched his audition on tape, he had taped it in New York and a few weeks went by, and we actually offered the role to another actor, a very good actor but someone who in retrospect wouldn't have been quite right." When the actor in question took a role in a Will Smith movie, Cuba pushed the producers to take a second look at Pascal's audition, after they had seen multiple candidates for the role over a course of three weeks. Brancato and his fellow producers were impressed.

"We were like, 'Wow, this guy's actually really good,'" Brancato recalls. "So, we hired him on a Friday and that Sunday night was the episode of *Game of Thrones* where he gets killed by that giant dude and on Monday morning IMDB had these little star meters and Pedro Pascal was the number one star in the world that week. And I adore that guy—he's a great actor and he

ABOVE: One of the aspects of set decoration involved creating detailed crime boards.

"HE WAS REALLY GOOD
AT WALKING BOTH SIDES
OF THE STREET"

CARLO BERNARD

just brings something to that role that's awesome."

While Boyd Holbrook's Steve Murphy shows some vivid shades of gray as his character struggles with the costs of the fight against the cartel, Peña is introduced as a character already somewhat compromised and at home with the constant corruption and slippery morality of law enforcement in Colombia. The show's writers worked with the real Peña to flesh out this portrait. "Javier would not mind me saying, in his younger days, Murphy used to call Peña, who was single, a 'man-slut,'" Brancato says. "So, we took inspiration from that." A *Miami Herald* newspaper article that suggested Peña had operated or allowed Los Pepes was a largely untrue if not outright defamatory of the DEA agent. But the idea of Peña's loyalties being tested between the DEA and the usefulness of Los Pepes against the Medellín cartel was an appealing one that Brancato definitely wanted to work into the series. "I was really interested in the notion that let's take this guy who is Mexican-American and has been down in Colombia for a year and a half before Murphy gets there, and let's have him be a little bit more rough and tumble, a little bit more Colombian-style in terms of his attitude and outlook about fighting these guys."

Part of the gray moral shading of the character of Peña was derived from the way he was willing to strike deals with some of the very forces he was attempting to bring to justice and play a long game that he reasoned would, in the end, help the DEA meet its goals in putting away Escobar and the Medellín cartel. With Los Pepes taking the fight to Escobar and showing results in ways the police and military in Colombia hadn't, Peña began to negotiate with elements of the vigilante group, knowing full well that Los Pepes had roots in the Cali cartel. Director Andrés Baiz says he felt it was important to add this dimension to Peña. "It was my idea to have Peña go and work with Los Pepes, because to kill a monster you have to become a monster yourself. And [the writers] said 'no, but he's our hero,' but you have to have the balance."

"Javier Peña always maintained that he didn't help Los Pepes," Bernard says. "I think in real life Javier Peña was the one American a lot of Colombians would talk to and the one a lot of Colombians felt an understanding with. He was really good at walking both sides of the street and on the show for dramatic purposes we have him be pulled a little bit further toward that side. Of course there are consequences and in season three the idea for Peña is that he's trying to redeem himself, hoping to find a little of the moral clarity in the hunt for Cali that he wasn't able to achieve in the hunt for Escobar."

ABOVE: Costume sketch created by cosume designer María Estela Fernández.

ABOVE: The many faces of Javier Peña.

THIS SPREAD: The DEA agents experienced some emotional moments in the offices.

DEA OFFICES

While most of the show is filmed on real locations, set designers Anthony Medina, Diana Trujillo (season one) and Salvador Parra (seasons two and onwards) had to construct standing sets for a few locations. The DEA offices were one of those few key sets that had to be built in order to authentically recreate the correct period look. This operational center became a home-away-from-home for Murphy and Peña and the scene of many important conversations and confrontations between the two men. Cinematographer Luis David Sansans worked with Parra to create a set that provided the cast with a range of atmosphere options for different scenes. "We tried to think how we could transform the atmosphere in that place. We had transitions everywhere, playing with dramatic environment and atmospheres when, for example, Boyd has to abandon his family. He's in this conflict in his mind and he's by himself at the office and there's just one single light on the desk just to create that atmosphere and that sadness for the character."

CREATING THE CONCEPTS

roduction designer Salvador Parra plans location shooting, construction, and set decoration down to the finest texture and detail, executing elaborate concept paintings of each setting before materials are purchased and set construction can begin. "I found that it was the only way I could trust my ideas in terms of color, my ideas in terms of texture," says Parra, "and if the crew doesn't know how strong the patinas, or the colors, or the tones should be, obviously the sets won't have the same power visually."

The set designer found that, although he was supervising the sets, scouting locations, and creating concepts, his designs encouraged a collaborative environment. "It becomes a very creative way to work with everyone because I receive more ideas from my crew."

The concept designs, as well as being beautiful pieces of artwork, really helped increase efficiency on set, "In this type of show we're moving so fast and there are so many sets," says Parra. "With these designs, the directors can prep before they get to the set because they already saw the concept a week or more before, so they know what they're going to find." His designs quickly became in high demand as an important stage in the set design process, "It's like trying to win a race getting all these concepts to the production."

BELOW: Location photos and detailed concept sketches by Salvador Parra demonstrate how much the production integrated his designs into the final sets.

THIS PAGE: A sketch by Salvador Parra (below) and a photo (above) from the final set of the ambassador's office.

PROFILE:
PABLO ESCOBAR

PATRON

PATRÓN

A native of Colombia born into the middle class (although fond of saying he came from poverty), Pablo Escobar rose from a life as a smuggler of marijuana and television sets to become one of the kingpins of the cocaine trade. He created a drug empire and became a figure of national prominence, a folk hero to the poor (many of whom he paid and bribed in order to keep them in his confidence). He was also a scourge to the police, army, and government: waging a reign of terror, bringing down airliners and government buildings to maintain his power. He then made a bargain to have himself jailed in a resort-like prison called *La Catedral* but saw his empire crumble and found himself a lonely, hunted man torn away from his family. Eventually his contact with his wife and children allowed the government to track him down and kill him.

Casting the role of Pablo Escobar was a pivotal challenge for the production—but José Padilha had someone in mind: Brazilian actor Wagner Moura, who had starred in Padilha's *Elite Squad* movies. Moura quickly agreed even though as a Brazilian native he mainly spoke Portuguese. However, Moura was determined to not only hone his Spanish, but to convincingly affect the appropriate regional accent for Escobar (this would prove a challenge not only for Moura, but for other members of the show's international cast).

In the hands of actor Wagner Moura and the show's writing staff, Pablo Escobar became one of the great characters in television history. A man of cold, uncontrollable fury, of unshackled ego and staggering wealth who nonetheless insisted on thinking of himself as a common man in league with the poor and unprotected people of Colombia. He was capable of unspeakable cruelty but was also devoted to his children, and a serial philanderer who took in mistresses and prostitutes by the dozens but still seemed to be in love with his wife. For Doug Miro, his fascination with the character extended to Escobar's vulnerability where his family was concerned. "It's entirely true that he was a man who was utterly devoted to his family," Miro says. "Despite the fact that he had this other life where he was a monster, killing people, and sleeping with other women, he really did love his wife and children. And doted on them and was constantly concerned with their security and was thinking about them nonstop, and we certainly accentuated that right up to the end."
In fact, Miro's, Bernard's, and Newman's plans for the drug lord 's downfall in the second season hinged on the dilemma between Escobar as criminal and Escobar as a family man.

ABOVE: Escobar in *La Catedral* with the stolen money (top) that sparked the deaths of Moncada and Galeano, and compiling his scrapbook (below.)

ABOVE: Escobar visits the jungle camp to make his first cocaine buy.

ABOVE: Escobar faces down a policeman shortly before his arrest.

ABOVE: A charming smile as he sends a teenager to his death.

"A lot of people know Pablo dies, so in a story like that, how do you invest people when you know the ending?" Bernard says. "For us it was so much about investing you in him as a human being and as a family man—how he sees the world and the possibility that maybe there's some hope for him and maybe this isn't it when he dies and maybe he'll be reunited with his family beforehand. Those smaller and larger tensions were really what we were working with at the end of the season. Hoping that you were just rooting for him even though part of you knows that he is a sociopath, and putting you in the shoes of a sociopath and exploring his hopes and fears was really strange."

Bernard says that much of Escobar's duality came out of research on the real man. "One of the jarring things about him, and you do read transcripts of his phone calls that were wiretapped or his talks with the press, he was always very solicitous, always has a sort of sense of humor, relatively good manners. And there's definitely a strong divergence between

that version of him that he presented and some of the acts that he perpetrated. The thing that was interesting about Escobar was that he was really relatable in that the things that drove him were obviously very human. He wanted to be accepted, there was a lot of corruption and inequity in Colombian life, and his desire to be loved and represent his particular aspect of Colombian society, which has been sort of overlooked and mistreated, was very relatable—he felt like an underdog and an outsider, he's born in a humble way, and there are lots of relatable aspects about him, but there at the same time are these incredible displays of monstrosity and mind-boggling cruelty. So as a viewer and a reader what was fascinating about him was the emotions were always very present—you understood him on one level but on another level, he was unfathomable in the actions he took. He was a human id acting out on the people around him in a way people understand but are also utterly shocked by."

MATEO "COCKROACH" MORENO

FACED WITH AN EPIC, MULTI-LAYERED storyline based on real history, the creators needed to introduce the larger-than-life character of Escobar and set the scene of the drug industry. The team of *Narcos* creatively positioned the Medellín cartel's initial chemist, Moreno (Luis Gnecco), as the audience's way into the story. An ordinary, money-grabbing man, Cockroach introduced Escobar to the manufacturing of cocaine. The ambitious Escobar, who had already established his own reputation as a ruthless smuggler, immediately saw the drug as a conduit to greater power and influence.

"HE WAS
UNFATHOMABLE IN
THE ACTIONS HE TOOK"

CARLO BERNARD

Doug Miro says Wagner Moura's performance was the key to creating sympathy in such a monstrous character. "I can't give enough credit to Wagner for forming that role, but also the amount of thought and time and energy he put into every detail of the performance. He was so thorough and thoughtful and questioning everything and making sure it felt true to who the character was, not just to who Escobar was, but to the character he had formed, because he really formed this rich, weird mixture of this guy who was both a sociopath and really an empathetic father and husband. That's so much due to Wagner's ability to engender both power and fear in one second and then a tremendous amount of empathy and love and humor in the next second. That ability to be able to switch between those two things is a really rare quality as an actor, and that's what makes his portrayal so powerful, because the design for him from the get-go was that he's a man who's torn between the demons of his violence and his ambition and his love for his family, and that's a great idea in the abstract but it needs to be executed on the page and beyond that you need a performer who can capture those things, and he did. Without him it wouldn't have had that mixture that made it so effective and tragic at the end."

Wagner Moura took on the role at the behest of José Padilha as the show geared up for production. "Padilha is a very important partner in my life," Moura says. "We had done the two *Elite Squad* films together. *Narcos* was also a great journey for both of us. Though I didn't speak Spanish nor looked like Pablo, he thought it would be important for him to have me around as we already had a very deep artistic connection."

Moura says that he, like many members of the *Narcos* cast and crew, recalls the real-life events that inspired the show, and worked ahead of filming to create an authentic depiction

of Pablo Escobar—albeit with a certain degree of artistic license. "I remember the image of Pablo dead on the rooftop. But the drug trade is a big deal in the whole world, especially in Latin America. This was a subject I was always interested in and *Narcos* gave me a chance to go deeper. I started six months before everybody else, flying by myself to Medellín to study Spanish and to live in Pablo's hometown. Also, I think in that time I read everything that was written about Pablo and modern Colombian history, though in the end of the day our Pablo Escobar is pretty much a creation. I studied a lot about the real Pablo in order to then forget it all and create my own version of him. Pablo wanted to be loved and to break through this immense social abysm that separates people in Latin American societies. The way he chose to do it was just horrible as he became a mass murderer. But he was just a man, a smart man, product of the environment he lived in. He was a family guy. All his biographies are very clear on that point. He loved his family. I had a lot of interest in that part of his personality."

BELOW: The series highlighted how dedicated Escobar was to his family.

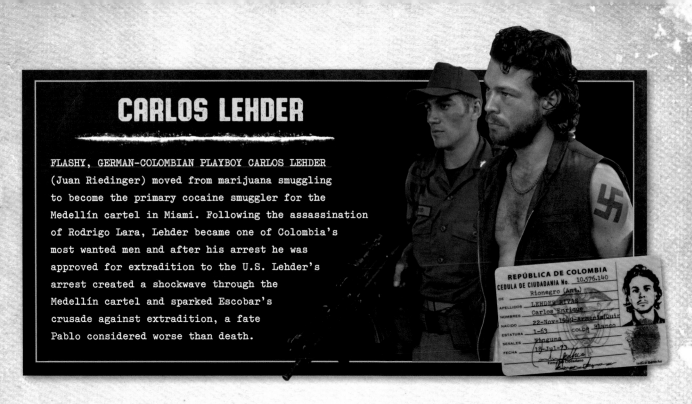

CARLOS LEHDER

FLASHY, GERMAN-COLOMBIAN PLAYBOY CARLOS LEHDER (Juan Riedinger) moved from marijuana smuggling to become the primary cocaine smuggler for the Medellín cartel in Miami. Following the assassination of Rodrigo Lara, Lehder became one of Colombia's most wanted men and after his arrest he was approved for extradition to the U.S. Lehder's arrest created a shockwave through the Medellín cartel and sparked Escobar's crusade against extradition, a fate Pablo considered worse than death.

Moura tackled and made his own many of the series' key moments, such as his enraged murder of Kiko Moncada and Fernando Galeano at *La Catedral*. "We discussed a lot about Pablo's reasons to kill those guys," Moura says. "I love working with Andi Baiz. We stayed together, living in a little house in the week we shot '*La Catedral*,' so there was a lot of discussion about everything. Andi is a major creative force in *Narcos*, plus he's Colombian and knew that story really well." Moura says he was also fond of the scenes of Escobar interacting with his father Abel on their farm near the end of the second season. "Alfredo Castro is an actor that I admire a lot. I was eager to work with him. That's a different episode, again directed by Andi. It is as if for a moment Pablo could imagine a different life for himself. It's sort of a Freudian episode."

Moura found the entire experience an important one. "It was a great journey in my life. It gave me a very strong political and social understanding on South America and therefore a better understanding of myself. Also, I'm now 100% sure that the drug policies are fundamentally wrong. They were clearly created as a way to impose social control over minorities. Repression is still killing and incarcerating Latin and black people all over the world, especially in the countries that produce and export drugs. This has to change."

BELOW: Escobar and his lawyer, Fernando Duque, discuss extradition.

PABLO'S FINCA NO.3

Although Escobar's drug money purchased him a grand estate, the infamous Hacienda Nápoles, he also owned numerous other homes to which he could travel or escape over the course of his drug career. Production designer Salvador Parra decorated several locations to represent these dwellings. "For me that was one of the toughest jobs in the stories, doing all of those mansions of Escobar, which were not mansions—they were called *fincas*," Parra said. The production designer noted that the challenge in outfitting the *fincas* was not to reflect Escobar's personality, but rather that of their former owners.

"For me Pablo Escobar is not a Scarface type of guy in a wonderful mansion with gold and marble columns—maybe that was in the first season, but in the second, Pablo is a humble guy who wants to be with his own *sicario*s and his own people. He wants to be with the poor people, but he lives in these great *fincas* and he just makes these people an offer they can't refuse and tells them, 'You get out of here now.' So those houses, there is no personality of Pablo in them and that was the main feeling of the dressing. It's not about Pablo, it was about who was there before."

BELOW: A final image from the set of Pablo's *finca* and a sketch by Salvador Parra.

ABOVE: Photos from the set (top) and a full-color concept design by Parra.

ESCOBAR ELECTED TO CONGRESS

One of the incredible-yet-true aspects of the *Narcos* story is Pablo Escobar's election to congress in 1982. Unsatisfied with simply being a powerful drug lord, Escobar ran for public office (a city council seat in Medellín) and had sufficient ambition to run for congress. It's a testament to both the drug lord's belief in his own destiny and his desire to be loved that to him, political office was entirely compatible with his role in the drug trade. Colombia's political system was also vulnerable enough to corruption that Escobar was able to easily bribe his way into a position as substitute to Jairo Ortega, who had agreed to resign immediately after being elected in order to give Escobar his seat in the House of Representatives. The position would have made Escobar immune from prosecution for any of the crimes that he had committed—the beginnings of what would become Escobar's obsessive, life-long quest to avoid extradition and responsibility for the violence and destruction he perpetrated.

The parliament sequence was filmed at the real location at Bolivar Square, with the grand hall of congress lending its own history and authenticity to the shoot. The episode 'The Men of Always' also marks the one and only occasion to bring Escobar, Murphy and Peña together in the same scene.

ABOVE: Valeria used her audience with the Colombian public to help boost Pablo's profile.

PROFILE:
VALERIA VELEZ

Pablo Escobar's mistress for over a decade, Valeria Velez (Stephanie Sigman) engaged in a mutually beneficial relationship with Escobar. She presented him to Colombia as the Robin Hood-like man of the people Escobar imagined himself to be while hyping ratings and circulation for her own journalistic career. She also enjoyed a catty relationship with rival journalist and ex-presidential daughter Diana Turbay. "She's modeled after a real character, a woman who had an affair with Escobar, was a TV journalist, and caused some sensation here and there," says Chris Brancato. "We fictionalized her name and we had actually considered Stephanie Sigman, the actress who plays her, we had her pegged on our board to play Tata and then José said, 'I think she should be the sexy reporter,' which again was a great call because she was perfect in that role and Paulina [Gaitán] was perfect as Tata."

BELOW RIGHT: A sketch by Salvador Parra of the iconic news van and a photo of the final vehicle used in the series.

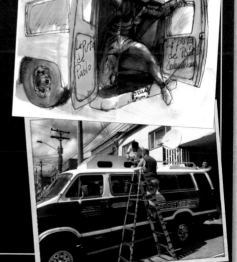

VALERIA'S VAN

VALERIA VELEZ WAS ESCOBAR'S ILLICIT lover, publicist, and political enabler in her role as a popular television journalist, but her ties to Escobar led to her assassination along with her news team. Valeria's news van had been her calling card as she covered Escobar's political rise, but it became the bloody site of her assassination at the hands of Los Pepes, its doors scrawled over with vengeful slogans as the bodies of Velez and her news crew lay inside.

PUSHED OUT OF POLITICS

ABOVE: A defeated Escobar says goodbye to his political dreams.

BELOW: Lara in possession the mugshot that would be the end to Escobar's political career.

scobar appeared in congress for the first time in 1983—what he believed was the height of his public respectability—to support the congressman openly accused by Rodrigo Lara of associating with the cartels. But in the chamber, the drug lord was accused by Lara of drug trafficking and left in disgrace.

Wagner Moura's legendary, slow burn performance as Escobar really ignited here as Escobar was humiliated at the hands of what, to Pablo, was a member of the upper class. Denied what he saw as almost his divine right as a common "man of the people," Pablo turned to deadly revenge.

MINISTER OF JUSTICE:
RODRIGO LARA

ONE OF THE FIRST FEW men willing to stand up to Pablo Escobar, Rodrigo Lara (Adan Canto) represented a rare, positive view of a politician - principled, brave, and incorruptible. Lara was a key example of the creators' desire to accurately depict the Colombian heroes at the center of the drug war. Immune to bribery and fearless in the face of Escobar, Lara exposed Escobar's criminality and barred his entry into congress, an act that would ultimately cost the Minister of Justice his life. Lara fell victim to Pablo's narco-terrorism, which was one of the tent pole moments of the show's transition towards a darker tone and suspense. When he was appointed ambassador to Czechoslovakia and prepared to flee the country, Lara was gunned down by Escobar's gunmen.

PROFILE:
THE AMBASSADORS

The ambassador character was a superior to Murphy and Peña who marshaled U.S. resources and often decided how far the two DEA officers could go in their pursuit of the Colombian cartels. They helped to highlight the unusual position of DEA agents attempting to enforce U.S. laws in foreign countries. The first ambassador, Noonan (Danielle Kennedy) became a popular character on the show, and an opportunity to portray a woman of power in the testosterone-heavy environment of the DEA and the cartels. "She's definitely a superior, kind of the be-all-and-end-all abroad," Carlo Bernard says. Arthur Crosby (Brett Cullen) took over for Ambassador Noonan under the administration of George H.W. Bush. Crosby was a U.S. Navy veteran who represented Bush's tougher stance on foreign narcotics. "That was interesting because in the Escobar story, you realize the fact that a new administration comes in, and that may mean a realignment in foreign policy," Carlo Bernard says. "It may mean the ambassador who's currently serving may be swapped out for an ambassador from the new guy's party, and in the case of the hunt for Escobar, they thought they were closing in and then the Clinton administration came in. So it was fascinating to realize how complex these stories are—it's not just a case of finding a guy and putting handcuffs on him."

BELOW: (Left) Ambassador Noonan. (Right) Ambassador Crosby.

PROFILE:
PABLO'S SICARIOS

Pablo Escobar commanded the loyalty of a group of *sicarios*, or hit men, who would take on his dirty work with a sense of camaraderie. In the series, these *sicarios* were amalgams of various people who had, at one point or another, worked for Escobar.

ROBERTO RAMOS "POISON"

One of the Medellín cartel's hit men, Poison (Jorge A. Jimenez) attempted to intimidate DEA Agent Murphy and his wife at their apartment by strangling their cat and leaving it for the couple as a warning. Ramos was then killed during a raid on a club by the Search Bloc and Colonel Carrillo, based on a tip from Steve Murphy. This was another step in the DEA agent's moral unraveling as he knowingly set up the *sicario* for death in payback for Poison terrorizing Murphy and his wife.

JUAN DIEGO DIAZ "LA QUICA"

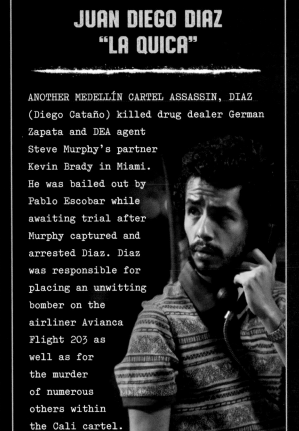

ANOTHER MEDELLÍN CARTEL ASSASSIN, DIAZ (Diego Cataño) killed drug dealer German Zapata and DEA agent Steve Murphy's partner Kevin Brady in Miami. He was bailed out by Pablo Escobar while awaiting trial after Murphy captured and arrested Diaz. Diaz was responsible for placing an unwitting bomber on the airliner Avianca Flight 203 as well as for the murder of numerous others within the Cali cartel.

NELSON HERNÁNDEZ "BLACKIE"

A LOYAL SUPPORTER OF ESCOBAR from his humble smuggler beginnings, Nelson Hernández "Blackie" (Julián Díaz) would take on any task to help his boss: he murdered the guerrilla members after their attack on the palace, helped Escobar maintain his hold over the drug world from *La Catedral*, and was pivotal in the death of Kiko Moncada. But after placing a car bomb in the center of Medellín on Escobar's orders led to dozens of deaths, the people of Medellín — and Blackie — started to turn against Escobar's violent ways. The *sicario* was picked up by the police and surrendered his phone in return for lesser charges, leading to La Quica's arrest.

JUNGLE CAMPS

With Colombia's vast cultural history and variety of tropical environments, the creators had the chance to include jungle camps in their list of diverse locations. Production designer Salvador Parra wanted to give the camps a sense of identity and history. Specifically, Parra wanted to suggest that the houses and villages had been stolen from their original owners by FARC or the paramilitiaries, and that innocents had lost their lives and property to the armed struggle between these two groups. "For those camps, I wanted to dress it and to make them believe that was a real village with real people who are not there anymore, like a ghost village," says Parra. One example was the jungle camp of M-19, which was supposed to be a paramilitary location, so it was decorated with weapons and anti-communist graffiti. "In my research, in every wall of those towns that were captured by these guys they have writing just to instill in the minds of their own soldiers so they can commit the most horrible crimes. So for me that had to be a very strong camp with all these legends on the walls with all this writing, with all these weapons and power and obviously supported by the American government."

THIS PAGE: Final photos from the sets and (below) a detailed sketch by Salvador Parra.

PROFILE:
ELISA ALVAREZ

Elisa is a fictional character based on various members of the M-19 communist guerrillas that waged war against the Medellín cartels. A Colombian student and communist, Elisa (Ana de la Reguera) was in a relationship with M-19 co-leader Alejandro Ayala. After being involved in some of the group's most notorious exploits, she became an informer who helped Murphy and Peña avoid attacks from Escobar's men. Alvarez is another example of the show's morally gray characters—her initial involvement in theft and kidnapping was balanced by her assistance to the DEA agents and her befriending of Murphy's wife, but she also became romantically involved with Peña. Pena's involvement with informants was always messy and it culminated in season three—with his failed and tragic attempt to cultivate Christina Jurado, as an informant.

BELOW: A board displaying photos of known communists from the Department of Justice.

PROFILE:
JORGE & FABIO OCHOA

REPÚBLICA DE COLOMBIA
CEDULA DE CIUDADANIA No. 10.681.003
DE ___Medellín (Ant.)___
APELLIDOS ___OCHOA VÁSQUEZ___
NOMBRES ___Jorge Luis___
NACIDO ___30-Sep-1950-Medellín(Ant.___
ESTATURA ___1-70___ COLOR ___Trig.___
SEÑALES ___Ninguna___
FECHA ___5-Feb-71___
Firma del Ciudadano
REGISTRADOR NACIONAL DEL ESTADO CIVIL
Indice Derecho

Jorge (André Mattos) and Fabio (Roberto Urbina) were some of the founding members of the Medellín cartel. They fell in with Escobar and José Gacha and created the Death to Kidnappers movement after the abduction of their sister Marta and eventually helped Escobar and his men fight extradition. Although the Ochoa brothers were the founders of the Medellín cartel Escobar soon eclipsed them, and even though they assisted Escobar by creating the Death to Kidnappers movement, they also undermined him in real life by surrendering to the government. "They make a deal to surrender ahead of Escobar," Brancato says. "They cut a deal with the Colombian government that they would do very little jail time and would be prosecuted for importing bulls from Spain or something innocuous in return for quitting the cocaine business, because they had gotten very wealthy. There were actually three Ochoa brothers and when I was writing the pilot I was thinking to have to divide lines between these three guys, and they weren't going to be absolutely central characters as part of the Medellín cartel, so I thought, 'Let's do two of them,' and in describing them, one of my favorite things was the comparison to Goldilocks—Cockroach was looking for who he should introduce this cocaine to and the Ochoa brothers are too soft and Gacha's too hard and Escobar is just right."

MARINA OCHOA

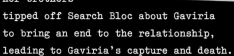

THE FICTIONAL YOUNGER SISTER OF Jorge and Fabio Ochoa, Marina Ochoa (Laura Perico) had no direct involvement in the drug operations of her brothers, but she was happy to spend her brothers' money on her own lavish lifestyle, and she also shared some of her brothers' ruthlessness. After she became involved in an affair with Pablo Escobar's married cousin Gustavo Gaviria, she suggested that Gustavo have Escobar arrange the death of Gustavo's wife so that she and Gaviria will no longer have to hide their affair. Instead, her brothers tipped off Search Bloc about Gaviria to bring an end to the relationship, leading to Gaviria's capture and death.

LEFT: Jorge in the first meeting with the Medellín cartel. BELOW: Fabio dares to question Pablo's judgement.

PROFILE:
HORACIO CARRILLO

olombian Army Colonel Carrillo was head of the police's Search Bloc unit who gradually earned a reputation for ruthlessness all but equal to that of the drug lords he fought, making Carrillo one of the only men the cartels truly feared. But Carrillo's risk-taking and confrontational tactics ended with his violent death when one of his raids led to an ambush by Pablo Escobar himself, who personally executed Carrillo.

The creation of Carrillo, a memorable but completely fictional character in the series, came about due to the need to incorporate some questionable aspects of the real-life model for the character, Hugo Martinez, into the show. "We wanted Carrillo to be a highly morally-compromised character but one with a certain dignity," says Chris Brancato. "And so, at first,

to be honest, the model was Martinez, and I even spoke to Martinez on the phone with a translator very briefly. But there were a couple of things going on. We didn't have his life rights, and a couple of things I wanted the character to do, potentially, not only did Martinez *not* do those things, it was potentially defamatory in my opinion to call the character Martinez and have him do these things. So Carrillo was a fictional character— José and I were at Sunset Gower Studios walking to a restaurant and I said, 'We need a name for this fictional character,' and I literally stepped on a star on the sidewalk that was for Leo Carrillo, a famous film director from the thirties or something, and José said, 'How about Carrillo? That sounds Colombian.'"

Actor Maurice Compte brought a quiet power to the character that made his death at the hands of Escobar all the

"WE WANTED CARRILLO TO BE A HIGHLY MORALLY-COMPROMISED CHARACTER"

CHRIS BRANCATO

more shocking. "I had done a pilot for F/X, the very first year F/X came into being, that unfortunately competed against *The Shield* and lost, and it was called *Dope*," Brancato says. "It was about drug trafficking in Los Angeles and it turned out to be a very good pilot and one of the better scripts I've ever written, and F/X couldn't decide which of the shows to pick up and they went with *The Shield*, so Dope was the one that got away.

The actor who played a bad guy in *Dope* was Maurice Compte, so lo and behold we're looking for someone to play Carrillo and we started off looking for actors of some note in South America. We're looking at like fifty, fifty-five, sixty-year old guys and we were kind of frustrated because they all felt kind of familiar, and then Eric and I were talking and we thought what if the guy was younger? So Carmen plays the tape of this guy reading very dry and very matter-of-fact and I thought this guy seems familiar, where do I know this guy from? And then I realized it's the guy from *Dope*, Maurice. I feel like now with *Narcos* I'm getting the chance to do this subject matter I really like and the idea that [Maurice] could come back and be part of it is like kismet to me. So he came back and was great."

BELOW: Carrillo and his men on the hunt for Gacha.

AERIAL PHOTOGRAPHY

Cinematographer Luis David Sansans, who joined the production in season two, says the combination of technology and the rich location possibilities helped raise the bar for the look of the show. "I used to be a helicopter fan because we didn't have drones at that time, and the experience I had with drones before *Narcos* was a disaster because they crashed. But for the show we use drones for everything—you can fly it over a city, and it's a great tool because you can do several things that you can't with helicopters—you can get at shots or places where helicopters can't go. I love Colombia and I really enjoyed the experience of shooting there—the people are really nice, and they were prepared already because of season one. They didn't have that experience in big projects like this and I think in season one they had a hard time because they had to teach them in a certain way how things would work for a show of this magnitude.

And I landed with all the system already prepped and ready to go, and I worked with a Brazilian gaffer, Marcelo Oliveira, who is amazing. I found my right hand right away and we had the same place for lighting and we clicked right away, so that was very helpful for me. So I landed in clouds."

The use of drone photography allowed not only for startlingly smooth, almost unreal aerial views of the Colombian countryside and cityscapes, but also for Steadicam-like overhead shots of street action and foot chases. "I remember being really fascinated and inspired by José's movies and *City of God*," Brancato says. "I just loved those big aerial shots where you're chasing through this really colorful slum. Shooting in Colombia was really the ticket because it just made the show feel very different and made it feel like you were really in a world. In the Gacha death scene we used drones over those banana fields which was fantastic."

ABOVE: Some of the breathtaking aerial photography used in the show.
BELOW: The creative team used drones to capture chase scenes through the streets.

POLICE ACADEMY

In the second season Murphy, Peña, and the DEA operation moved to Medellín and the heart of the police training center, where both exterior troop formations and assemblies took place along with interior meeting spaces, the latter of which were constructed on a sound stage. "I wanted it to feel like very old construction from the forties or fifties," production designer Salvador Parra said. "It was an institution from Colombia that was corrupted and they're trying not to be corrupt anymore because of the terrible situation with the cartels. So the construction is a little art deco, but art deco in a Colombian way and governmental style— we used a lot of tiles, all the columns are very strong structures made of concrete." Parra and his crew had to work to create not only an impression of reality, but the illusion that the space was larger than the stage available. "That set is really handmade—every tile in that set was handmade and we painted the whole thing. Colombia doesn't have a huge soundstage so we used one of the biggest stages in Colombia, but it was for TV, not for movies—we had a lot of depth in that stage but we used every inch and little space of the set to make it as big as we could and to make it feel like these guys were little cockroaches inside this building."

BANDERA
POLICIA NACIONAL
BANDERA COLOMBIANA
EN BUCLES.

PROFILE:
JOSÉ GACHA

ABOVE: Gacha wasn't afraid to go up against Escobar.

ABOVE: The founding of the Medellín cartel.

Although born in Colombia, José Gacha was known as "the Mexican" because he affected Mexican style headgear and clothing along with other cultural artifacts at his compound. He became one of the most powerful players in the Medellín cartel. He partnered with the Ochoa brothers and Carlos Lehder and rarely hesitated to murder both rivals and associates who threatened his power. Gacha was involved in the 1984 assassination of Minister of Justice Rodrigo Lara and amassed a cache of formidable defensive weapons including a rocket launcher. Flushed out from their ranch at Cartagena by Colonel Carrillo and the Search Bloc, Gacha and his son Freddy were pursued by Search Bloc helicopters in their pickup truck and killed under the orders of Agent Javier Peña in 'Explosivos.'

In real life Gacha very nearly suffered an even more spectacular demise: when he was traced to his mountaintop *finca* by the nascent radio surveillance program Centra Spike, the Colombian government ordered a bombing raid on the compound by fighter jets from the Colombian air force. With the aircraft closing in on their target, the raid was called off at the last second when one of the pilots realized that a small village located adjacent to Gacha's compound would likely have been destroyed by the missile fire.

Puerto Rican actor Luis Guzmán (*Traffic, Punch Drunk Love*) was probably one of the few faces on the show familiar to American audiences when *Narcos* debuted in 2015—but familiar for English-speaking roles in American movies. "The cast were from all of the different countries in South America," Chris Brancato notes, "which of course bothers some Spanish speakers because the accents aren't always perfect Colombian. For Gacha, we had a meeting with the Mexican actor Eugenio Derbez, one of the biggest stars in Mexico, and I think because he's so outrageous that we saw the role as one that almost had an edge of comedy to it. Derbez is a very famous comic actor and we met with him and it became quickly apparent that his own shooting schedule would never allow for him to do it. I remember talking with José and I don't know how Luis's name came up but I remember José looking at his picture and saying, 'I love this guy!' and me agreeing. But Luis got the script in English and read it and accepted the role and flew to Colombia and on his first day there he got a packet with call sheets and restaurants in Colombia and the shooting draft of the script, and he went back to his room to read his scenes and thought, 'Oh my god, all my scenes are in Spanish.' He didn't realize until he got there that he was going to speak Spanish in the show."

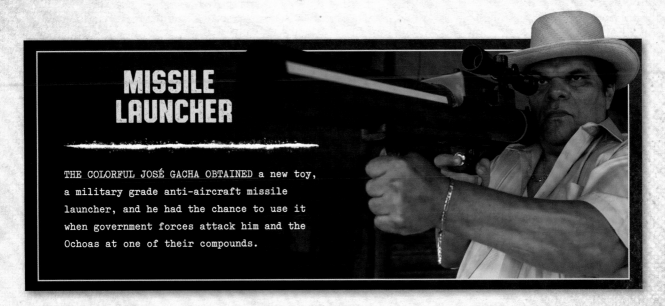

MISSILE LAUNCHER

THE COLORFUL JOSÉ GACHA OBTAINED a new toy, a military grade anti-aircraft missile launcher, and he had the chance to use it when government forces attack him and the Ochoas at one of their compounds.

PROFILE:
JAIME CARRERA

A young street courier hustling to provide for his wife, Natalie, and their newborn daughter, Jaime Carrera (German De Greiff) became a pawn in the bombing of Avianca Flight 203. This was the beginning of an all-out war by Pablo Escobar against the state and an act so cruel in its execution and so monstrous in scale that it placed Escobar on the world stage as a terrorist. This was also the beginning of a series of events, from kidnappings to street bombs, that put the Colombian government and people collectively with their backs against the wall. Colombia was eventually willing to accept any compromise—no matter how outrageous— to stop the bloodshed Escobar and the cartel caused.

Escobar's cold execution of this plot reflected his false projection of himself as a hero for the common man. He seemingly invited Jaime not just into the cartel, but into his family for a position of importance. He even visited Jaime and Natalie at their modest home where he praised the beauty of their infant daughter, assuring Natalie that he was about to provide for their every need before putting Carrera on the plane with a tape recorder that had been rigged by Efram Gonzalez to explode. The target of the assassination attempt was not on the plane, leaving the flight's 110 victims dead for no advantage to either side in the drug war. "I had read—and you don't know if this is absolutely verified or not—that an unwitting guy had been sent up to that plane and had blown it up without knowing what he was doing, which obviously is the most horrifying thing in the world," Chris Brancato says. "It was not absolutely sure that Escobar did it although he was blamed for it immediately afterward. I think we just thought that Escobar did use these slum kids to do all kinds of murderous stuff so we found that beautiful faced kid and it just really shows the monstrosity of Pablo Escobar."

In the aftermath of the bombing and Jaime's death, Escobar caused even more bloodshed when he sent *sicario* Poison and his crew to kill Natalie and eliminate any witnesses to the plot. Murphy and Peña arrived too late to save Natalie, but they found that the Carrera's baby had survived the shooting— and a shell-shocked Murphy took the infant home to his wife Connie.

EXPLOSIVOS

IN 'EXPLOSIVOS,' ESCOBAR ARRANGED for a drug courier to detonate an explosive device on Avianca Flight 203 in an attempt to assassinate Colombian president César Gaviria.

While the production often used sophisticated effects to integrate digital aircraft into its aerial photography, it was always the intention to focus on the innocence of the Jaime Carrera character in the context of the airline bombing, rather than on a spectacular visual effect of the aircraft's explosion. The following episode, 'You Will Cry Tears of Blood,' showed actual news footage of the aftermath of the crash shots of body bags being moved, their inhabitants smashed into shapeless masses by the impact of the crash,

in what remains one of the most disturbing moments of the series. While *Narcos* did not depict any of its characters in Colombia using cocaine, the brutal impact of the drug on Colombian society is a constant drumbeat in the series.

ABOVE: The explosive device hidden inside a suitcase.
NEXT SPREAD: Pablo visits Jaime at his home.

"IT JUST REALLY SHOWS THE MONSTROSITY OF PABLO ESCOBAR"

CHRIS BRANCATO

ABOVE: A sombre moment at Galan's funeral, shortly before Gaviria agreed to run for office.

resident of Colombia, Gaviria (Raúl Méndez) made the war against Pablo Escobar and the drug cartels a key element of his presidency, but political realities and Escobar's popular clout sometimes forced the president into uncomfortable compromises. Gaviria as president eventually made the deal to imprison Escobar at *La Catedral*, suffered politically during a hostage crisis at the prison, and finally saw Escobar killed by government forces. For the series, Gaviria represented another complex Colombian hero, one struggling to follow his own moral compass in the face of structural inertia, internal corruption, and the very real threat of violence and death at the hands of Escobar and the cartel.

"In the case of Gaviria, he was a guy who never really wanted to become president," says Carlo Bernard. "After the assassination of [Luis Carlos Galán] who he was campaign manager for, Gaviria basically stood up and said, 'I'll do this,'

and he wasn't necessarily cut out emotionally and personality-wise to be a politician. But he did it out of a sense of duty and for us that was really interesting, to see how a guy like that also has to deal with the moral complexities of wanting to stop the bloodshed. In the first season he cuts a deal that some people were angry about, but then after Escobar escapes *La Catedral* there are no deals to be made—they're going to hunt this guy down and kill him. So, for us I think he was a very sympathetic and compelling character who represented a small window on the complicated and heroic nature of the Colombian story. He had to deal with the Americans demanding results but not necessarily having to deal with the consequences, whereas Colombians did have to deal with the consequences which put him in a delicate spot. You have to broker the Americans' cooperation but by the same token you, and the people you represent, are going to live with the consequences of it."

"HE HAD RESILIENCE AND HE WAS BRAVE IN MANY RESPECTS"

ANDRÉS BAIZ

Director Andrés Baiz says that Gaviria is better regarded now than he was during his time in office. "I actually think Gaviria is one of those presidents that history has redeemed. When he was president there was a lot of pressure on him and he was seen as making, probably, more mistakes than he actually did, but now looking back on history he's seen as a good president that had probably one of the toughest years in Colombia's recent history. Most of his decisions were the correct ones—of course there were failures: letting Pablo have *La Catedral*, this luxury club where he was incarcerated—but apart from that he was really trying to combat this huge menace that the country had and also dealing with so much corruption in the military and the police forces. He had resilience and he was brave in many aspects, and he was brave in the sense that he was a human being—a person that had doubts, that questioned himself, that he was alone in the middle of all of this. So I admire him, and we do a good portrayal of him in that kind of dubious scenario: 'I'm not a hero but I'm trying to do my best and there's so much to consider.' I love the fact that we dealt so much with politics in the first two seasons and having the chance as a director to portray the history of my own country in that regard."

LUIS CARLOS GALÁN

LUIS CARLOS GALÁN (JUAN PABLO ESPINOSA) pulled the ultimate tripwire when he made a speech calling for extradition of the narcos to the U.S. He was a popular politician and a crusader against the drug trade but he wasn't invincible. Extradition being the one thing that Escobar truly feared, Pablo had Galán assassinated, producing an outpouring of public grief. His death changed the course of the first season as it motivated César Gaviria to pursue the presidency and also reinforced Escobar's determination to fight the Colombian government.

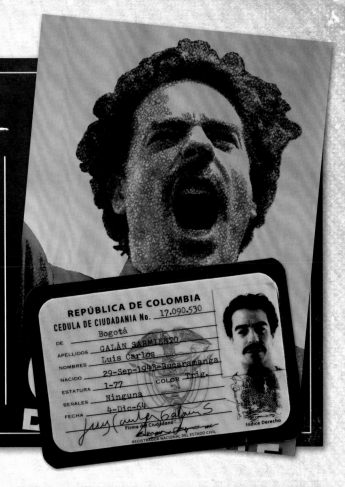

ABOVE: Props from the series: one of Galán's campaign posters and his identification card.

DESPERATE MEASURES

WHEN ESCOBAR COULDN'T FORCE THE President to agree to his demands he targeted the influential by kidnapping their children. "One of my favorite things to do is to title the episodes even if nobody ever sees it, and that one is based on an expression I heard which is, 'You will cry tears of blood,'" Chris Brancato says. "Which is, the way you really mess with someone is not to kill them but to kill their children. So that's a favorite episode of mine too because what a dastardly thing to do, and he brought them to their knees it was incredible that he did that and of course there was kind of a relationship between him and Turbay, and there's a very good scene and that actress (Gabriela de la Garza) is amazing, and so he obviously didn't want her to die. I don't think he intended to kill her and it was actually a police raid that killed her."

ABOVE: Gaviria and Sandoval at the funeral for Diana Turbay.

PRESIDENT'S OFFICE

The Colombian President's office presents a contrast to the gritty locale of the DEA offices. Production designer Salvador Parra also sought to reflect native architecture. "That was based on the real house of the president so we just tried to have this federalist architecture in his office, which was different and really the opposite from the DEA offices," Parra explained. "It looks more presidential and more clean with all the paintings and banners and heroes on the walls. But Gaviria is about an old structure that is falling down—the tiles are getting dark and the place, you can even smell it, like people are sweating there, so it's a completely different approach in terms of textures."

THIS SPREAD: Concept designs (below) by Salvador Parra and final set photos (above) of the national palace.

National Palace/Gaviria's Office
Parra 2015/Narcos

LA CATEDRAL

In another one of the show's difficult-to-believe but true developments, Escobar—determined to avoid extradition to the U.S.—made a deal with the Colombian government to serve five years in prison. Spread thin and beaten down by years of harrowing war with the cartel, the Colombian government were backed into an absurd bargain that allowed Escobar to have a prison built to his own specifications, allowing the drug lord to live in luxury and continue running his empire from prison. Even for the citizens of Colombia, jaded by years of corruption and compromise, this was a cruel joke that cost the government's reputation dearly—but this "bad peace" was seen by the president and his administration as preferable to a continuing war.

Recreating *La Catedral* was one of the creative team's biggest challenges, but season one production designers Anthony Medina and Diana Trujillo had abundant research on the real facility. "We were very fortunate in that we had photos that Steve Murphy had taken right after Pablo's escape," producer Jesse Rose Moore said. "He and Peña went to the prison so we recreated that moment. Right down to things like when Peña wears Pablo's Russian fur hat. And when we were designing the prison we tried to get details right."

Although the production designers successfully emulated the atmosphere and design of the infamous location, the scenes set in *La Catedral* weren't filmed in the actual facility. The real

BELOW: The pretence of a prison allowed Escobar to continue operations from behind "bars."

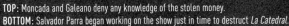

TOP: Moncada and Galeano deny any knowledge of the stolen money.
BOTTOM: Salvador Parra began working on the show just in time to destruct *La Catedral*.

"WHEN WE WERE DESIGNING THE PRISON WE TRIED TO GET THE DETAILS RIGHT"

JESSE ROSE MOORE

La Catedral had been transformed and wasn't available for filming so the team searched for a suitable replacement that they could use to faithfully recreate the prison. "The location that we found was a reform school that was no longer in use," Moore explained. "We needed a place that was big enough; we needed a place that we could turn into this sort of quasi-prison that he had; we needed a place that was remote enough, that was in the hills, and we shot that maybe an hour outside Bogotá."

Production designer Salvador Parra joined Narcos in season two, after the original *La Catedral* set had been designed and built. "It was amazing and it was like a palace inside," Parra explains. "They had everything there: billiard tables, bowling, prostitutes if they wanted, and Pablo has his own office and his own room with air conditioning and TVs, and it was like a luxury hotel—that was all established when I got there."

It was Parra's job to embellish its interior—and oversee its destruction—in the wake of Escobar's escape from the facility during an ill-advised government raid. "When we did the aftermath we tried to add more of these beer tables and more of the life that was going on there—that's how the second season starts and then I destroyed the whole thing," Parra said.

PRISON YARD MURDER

One of the key scenes in illustrating Escobar's volatility (and the lawlessness of his "prison" stay in *La Catedral*) is the drug lord's brutal slaying of his associates, a scene that ended with Escobar's face drenched in blood from his two victims. Director Andrés Baiz helmed the action. "That scene where he kills Moncada [Christian Tappán] and Galeano [Orlando Valenzuela] which is kind of a Greek trial in a sense, I think the acting there is superb—there is a moment before the killing where Moncada spits on Escobar and it was real spit and it was hanging from his nose—it was beautiful. But that's where the downfall of Escobar begins. If he didn't kill those two guys in prison then the government would never have gotten into *La Catedral* to take him out and he never would have fled."

Producer Chris Brancato remembers that he tried to provide an inciting incident that would set Escobar off from slow boil to killing rage, but it was unnecessary where actor Wagner Moura was concerned. "I was trying to come up with a reason why he kills these people, who are his lieutenants, that sets the stage for his ultimate downfall. The money that gets discovered was a true fact: there was some peasant who finds money buried and Escobar suspects that it's money that Moncada and Galeano stole from him, so there is foreshadowing, but I was pitching Wagner something specific that happens moments before he explodes. So for example I pitched a scene where his kid gets beat up at school and he tells his kid 'you have to fight' and he finds out his kid got beat up again, and I pitched some other thing, so I was looking for an onscreen specific reason why he explodes in anger and kills those guys. And Wagner says, 'You know, Chris, I don't think we need that, I think I can make it work without that, and I think it's gilding the lily to give such a specific reason.' At that point I thought, *if you say you can play it then I know you can*, and obviously he did. I was there the day they shot the pool cue scene and it was insane watching it be filmed and doing the reverse shot where the blood splashes onto his own face and it was really cool."

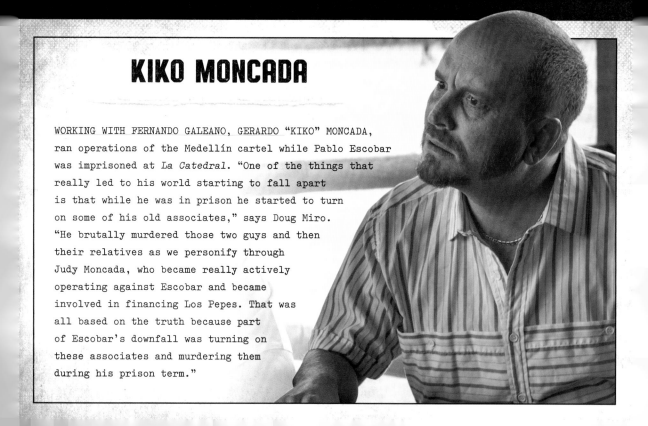

KIKO MONCADA

WORKING WITH FERNANDO GALEANO, GERARDO "KIKO" MONCADA, ran operations of the Medellín cartel while Pablo Escobar was imprisoned at *La Catedral*. "One of the things that really led to his world starting to fall apart is that while he was in prison he started to turn on some of his old associates," says Doug Miro. "He brutally murdered those two guys and then their relatives as we personify through Judy Moncada, who became really actively operating against Escobar and became involved in financing Los Pepes. That was all based on the truth because part of Escobar's downfall was turning on these associates and murdering them during his prison term."

ABOVE: A paranoid Escobar snaps.

BELOW: A reverse shot of the murder, showing Escobar's reaction.

PROFILE:
JUDY MONCADA

The vengeful widow of Kiko Moncada, Judy Moncada (Cristina Umaña) played a part in her husband's death by speaking out about the high taxes charged to her husband in front of Escobar (who never forgot a slight.) After killing Judy's husband, Escobar also killed her brother Jaime, and she eventually teamed up with the Castaños and the Cali cartel. "Escobar burned a lot of people," Carlo Bernard says. "Obviously, he hurt innocent persons like the people who lost children in bombings or the family members of allies that he betrayed, and Judy embodied that unleashed vengeance of a fellow trafficker."

Moncada was one of the instances in the series where the true story differs slightly from the narrative of the series. "It is true that, out of revenge, she wants to kill Escobar," explains Andrés Baiz. "But in reality, Judy wasn't the wife, she was the sister of Moncada." The viewers watched Judy evolve from being the out-

spoken wife of a narco to a power-hungry—and only female—drug lord in her own right. "This is a very testosterone driven show, and we sometimes don't have the strongest scenes for female actors," says Andrés Baiz. "So it's inspiring to see the Judy Moncada character who is tough, intricate, and smart, who's willing to go against Pablo Escobar. She's the villain of the villain." Producer Jesse Rose Moore adds, "She's very complicated, she's not a black and white character. She wasn't going to let Escobar get away with it, and she wasn't thinking about all the collateral damage she was causing as well. A lot of these characters tend to be very selfish."

The creative team credits the actress's portrayal for such a strong character, "Cristina Umaña, who plays Judy, is one of the best Colombian actors and we learned so much working with her—it was very enjoyable," says Andrés Baiz.

ABOVE: A stylish Judy Moncada in a sketch by María Estela Fernández.

MONCADA LABS

roduction designer Salvador Parra had previously worked on several film and television projects about narcos, so he had heavily researched the production of cocaine and the look and materials used in cocaine labs before starting on the series. "One of the hardest parts of the series was the cocaine labs because in almost every episode there was a cocaine lab," Parra said, noting that he wanted to show the progression of sophistication in the cartel's labs as they grew in wealth and power, starting from primitive labs in the Colombian jungle to high-tech facilities. "I think the Judy Moncada lab was like a little factory, so I wanted [to show] these guys were really getting very sophisticated. Every lab had to be different but it's the same process. In the Judy Moncada lab it was like

specific burners, electric burners for every process, different kinds of cocaine being processed, using all those different kinds of chemicals with labels instead of just the regular chemical containers that were in the jungle. Now you have beautiful crystal jars." Parra wanted to give viewers an idea of exactly how cocaine was made and processed. "You have to explain it visually. You have to understand that from that bucket there's some acid that goes inside and then they add potassium sulfide. After the incantation of that you have to heat it so all the acid becomes hydrochloric acid, so now we have cocaine. So I try to do it visually and that was part of the intention of all the cocaine labs, to make people understand the process."

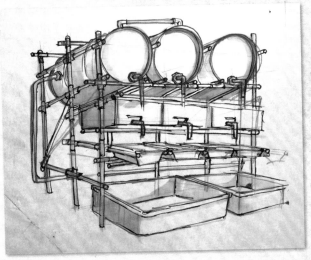

ABOVE: Judy Moncada surveys the damage to her lab after an attack.

TOP: A sketch of the lab equipment by Salvador Parra. **BOTTOM:** Kilos of cocaine.

concept sketches by S

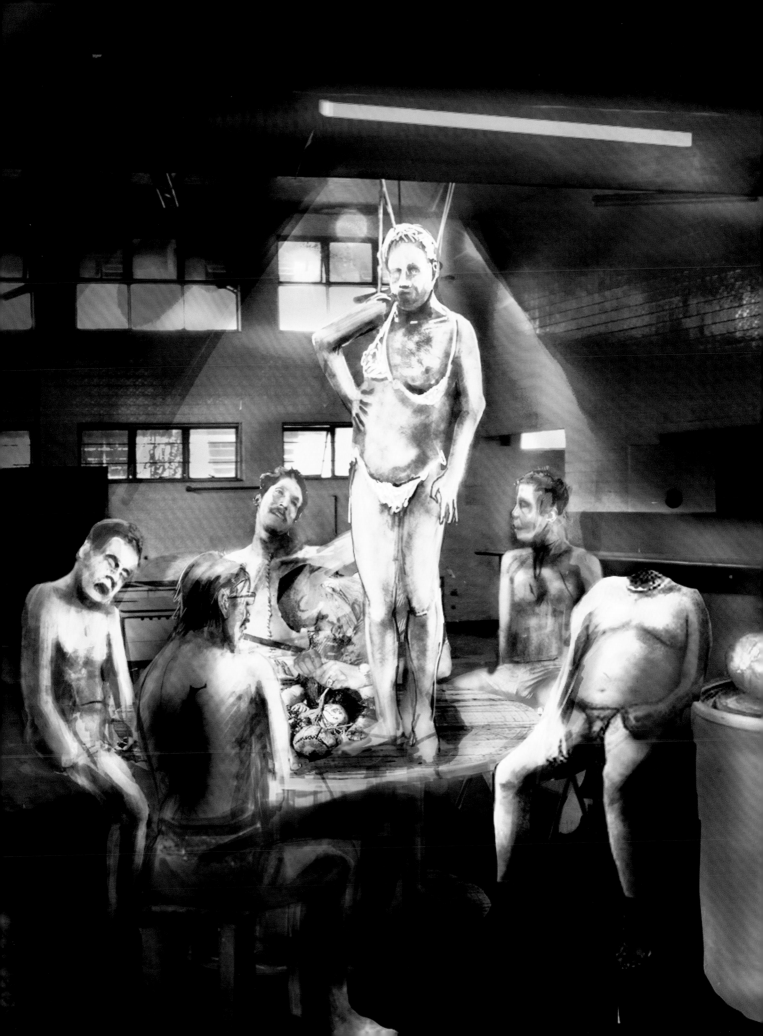

MONCADA COMPOUND

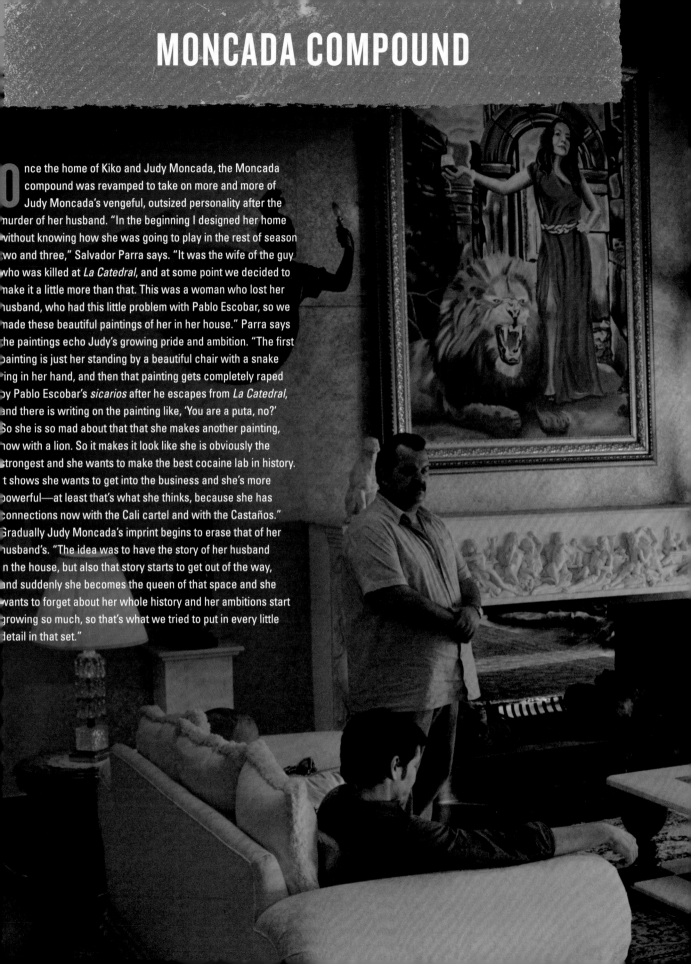

nce the home of Kiko and Judy Moncada, the Moncada compound was revamped to take on more and more of Judy Moncada's vengeful, outsized personality after the murder of her husband. "In the beginning I designed her home without knowing how she was going to play in the rest of season two and three," Salvador Parra says. "It was the wife of the guy who was killed at *La Catedral*, and at some point we decided to make it a little more than that. This was a woman who lost her husband, who had this little problem with Pablo Escobar, so we made these beautiful paintings of her in her house." Parra says the paintings echo Judy's growing pride and ambition. "The first painting is just her standing by a beautiful chair with a snake ring in her hand, and then that painting gets completely raped by Pablo Escobar's *sicarios* after he escapes from *La Catedral*, and there is writing on the painting like, 'You are a puta, no?' So she is so mad about that that she makes another painting, now with a lion. So it makes it look like she is obviously the strongest and she wants to make the best cocaine lab in history. It shows she wants to get into the business and she's more powerful—at least that's what she thinks, because she has connections now with the Cali cartel and with the Castaños." Gradually Judy Moncada's imprint begins to erase that of her husband's. "The idea was to have the story of her husband in the house, but also that story starts to get out of the way, and suddenly she becomes the queen of that space and she wants to forget about her whole history and her ambitions start growing so much, so that's what we tried to put in every little detail in that set."

A HOSTAGE SITUATION

One of the season's most suspenseful moments played out when President Gaviria's Vice Minister of Justice realized that the Colombian troops surrounding the prison had no intention of raiding the compound, and decided to enter and face Escobar by himself. Carlo Bernard explains. "In the aftermath of that he seemed to be unfairly caught up in the political backlash of the whole *Catedral* nightmare. It was all a scandal because, of course, people were outraged and it was kind of absurd, and I think he bore the brunt of that. That character was a little bit of an amalgamation, but based on a real guy who'd been given the ticklish job of having to go in and negotiate terms and was held hostage. There was a lot of confusion and chaos, and a bunch of generals looking for any way possible to pass the buck. This guy got himself in a sort of untenable and highly unappealing situation of being forced to go in there and try to get Escobar to give himself up."

Chris Brancato says the real-life subject is currently chief of security for one of Colombia's main airlines. "He came in to Colombia to sit with us—this was a part of our research: we also met with César Gaviria, I spoke to Hugo Martinez,

BELOW: Escobar's intimidation of the Vice Minister of Justice.

BELOW: Sandoval calls his superior for help.

"IT WAS BRAVE BUT STUPID AT THE SAME TIME"

ANDRÉS BAIZ

obviously Murphy and Peña—he sat there and told us, José and Eric, that Escobar offered him a Diet Coke, all kinds of these details. So that story is really authentic, and in retrospect the idea that he walked in there thinking that he could negotiate was obviously foolish."

It seemed that Escobar was about to finally pay the price and be put to justice as President Gaviria ordered an assault on *La Catedral* with the intent of rescuing Sandoval, capturing Escobar and his men, and relocating them to a genuine prison. But with the assistance of elements of the army who had been bought and paid for, Escobar escaped into the jungle as an end

to season one. "It's absurd in a way and that was very well researched from my part," Andrés Baiz says about the Sandoval character and his impact on the *La Catedral* standoff. "That episode was very much about his character, and he and Gaviria and everybody all said there were a lot of mistakes made, especially on the naïve side. He was very young, and he thought he was going to go in and be supported by the military and take Pablo out, but he undermined the whole situation. It was brave but stupid at the same time, and then Gaviria had to make the decision whether he should save his friend or not, so morally it was a very interesting episode."

PROFILE: LIMÓN

A former pimp and taxi driver in Medellín who became Pablo Escobar's right-hand man in the drug lord's final days, Limón (Leynar Gomez) was initially hired to secretly ferry Escobar in the trunk of his taxi to drug meetings in order to avoid government checkpoints. In one of the season's most poignant personal stories, Limón recruited his childhood friend, Maritza (Martina García) to ride along with him as a "taxicab passenger" while they transported Escobar. However, the "easy money" quickly devolved into physical danger and betrayal of trust and, ultimately, led to her death by Limón's hand.

The story of Limón and Maritza was one of many ways *Narcos* depicted the toll that the drug war took on ordinary Colombians—people who would have never intentionally become involved in the narcotics trade, but who found their involvement with the cartels unavoidable and could quickly find themselves in dangerous circumstances. Although the Limón backstory was crafted, in reality, Pablo did spend the end of his life with a driver named Limón. "They'd been living in fairly unglamorous and reduced circumstances, and this young kid—who was also killed by the police in the raid—had been with him in that last stretch of his fugitive run," says Carlo Bernard.

The creative team imagined how human nature would affect two people living together in such close quarters and wanted to express the intimacy that would have formed between the drug lord and his driver in that situation. "That just inspired us to find out who that guy was, what were those conversations like between some kid driver and Pablo Escobar? It's kind of just the two of them, who's making dinner on Tuesday night?" says Bernard.

ALTERNATIVE TRAVEL PLANS

Flushed from the luxurious prison facility of *La Catedral*, Escobar was forced to maintain a low profile and endure the indignity of being driven in the trunk of a taxicab to meet with his ongoing narcotic trafficking contacts. But while doing so Escobar found himself enjoying his fame and notoriety among the "common people" who he had always identified with and who he had lost contact with during his years as a high-profile man of wealth and power.

"That is something that Pablo would do," producer Jesse Rose Moore said. "He would travel by taxi while making his phone calls because it would be much harder for anyone to pinpoint his calls, and he could stay on the phone longer if he was moving because they couldn't track his location. Sometimes he would go in the trunk too, and he would also go out in disguises." Moore said that the scene of Escobar being surrounded by admirers in a Medellín neighborhood fed into the drug lord's belief in the country's poor as a powerful political base. "It appealed to his ego because he liked to think of himself as a hero to the people and didn't think about all the damage he left behind."

ABOVE: Escobar found his way around the city-wide man hunt.

RICARDO AND EDGAR PRISCO

A COLOMBIAN DENTIST AND MEMBER of the Medellín cartel, Ricardo Prisco (Federico Rivera) assisted Escobar in tracking and killing rival drug traffickers. After Escobar escaped from *La Catedral*, Ricardo became the drug lord's personal physician, prescribing him pharmaceuticals to help the beleaguered Escobar deal with high stress levels and fainting episodes, particularly after Pablo was forced to be separated from his family as they attempted to find sanctuary in Germany. Ricardo assisted Escobar by joining an attack on the Cali cartel at Montecasino, partnering with La Quica and Escobar's accountant Rojas to collect money from slum dwellers in debt to Pablo in Medellín in order to finance the assault. For his trouble, Ricardo was shot by one of his compatriots in the escapade who was reluctant to join the fight. Ricardo's younger and considerably less accomplished brother Edgar (Leonardo Garcia) made the mistake of too often using his brother's satellite phone to call Escobar while being monitored by the Centra Spike radio surveillance operation, leading to his death during a raid on a billiards room by Search Bloc.

PROFILE:
CARLOS AND FIDEL CASTAÑO

C arlos (Mauricio Mejía) and Fidel Castaño (Gustavo Angarita Jr.) formed the right-wing paramilitary group AUC to avenge the death of their father Jesus, who had been murdered by the communist FARC guerillas. Adamantly against any drug money funding the paramilitaries, Carlos was particularly infuriated by Escobar's funding of the M-19 communist group. Fidel was known as "El Rambo" for his aggressive command of troops in the AUC's battles with the communists. Producer Jesse Rose Moore said the production looked to cast actors who resembled the real-life brothers: "I think Maurice who played Carlos Castaño looks a lot like the real guy, and we thought [he and Gustavo Angarita Jr.] went together as brothers. They had different temperaments, which we needed: Carlos is a little more pushy and prone to violence and the older brother is a little quieter, but they're both killers."

With Cali godfathers Gilberto and Miguel Rodríguez and Medellín renegades Judy Moncada and Don Berna, the Castaño brothers formed Los Pepes to launch a combined opposition to the Medellín cartel. After six months of operation and with Escobar's organization decimated, Los Pepes disbanded and Gilberto Rodríguez graciously offered the Castaño brothers all of the cocaine they had taken during their raids on the Medellín cartel. At this point Carlos' bold anti-drug stance miraculously changed and he decided to go into the cocaine business in order to fund the AUC. The Castaños eventually found themselves exiled with Judy Moncada after Don Berna discovered that Judy was informing for the DEA against the cartel.

BURNING VILLAGE

Production designer Salvador Parra was able to graphically illustrate the activities of the Castaños and their paramilitaries by showing the remains of a village destroyed by the AUC. "Burning Village was supposed to be the opposite of M-19, the FARC," Parra says. "It was taken by the communists and then obviously these paramilitaries arrived and burned the whole town, because that was the type of message these guys used to send to make a statement." Parra said that in *Narcos* the Castaños are waging a personal war on the communists because their father was killed by M-19, but the look of the burning village was intended to tell a larger story. "In a sense I put a little of the history of the environment so we had much more information about these communities and how the situation is in Colombia in that moment of the story."

ABOVE AND RIGHT: Sketches by Salvador Parra.

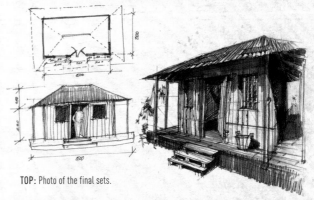

TOP: Photo of the final sets.

ABOVE: Concept sketch of Burning Village.

MONTECASINO

The base of operations for Los Pepes and the Castaño brothers, the estate of Montecasino was the target for a vengeful and desperate raid by Escobar after Los Pepes put the Medellín drug lord's back against the wall. "Montecasino is the place that is the bullpen for the Castaño brothers, a real place in Medellín," Salvador Parra said. "That's interesting in terms of production design because I decided to have a lot of taxidermy animals there, just because these guys are hunters and they're hunting Pablo Escobar now. I wanted to make it look like these guys are really dangerous and they know how to do their work, so they're going to catch Pablo. So the whole decoration was tiger heads and other terrible things just to give them the power of these guys in terms of hunting—what they want to do is hunt communists and hunt Pablo Escobar, and they get paid for that. Montecasino in reality was a very luxurious house with a lot of *caletas*, which is a place to hide money or to even hide yourself from the police or a Pablo Escobar attack or something like that."

ABOVE AND BELOW: The Castaño brothers liked to display their hunting trophies on the wall.

COLONEL CARRILLO KILLED

Colonel Carrillo was one of the few government or military figures who seemed as ruthless as Escobar and one of the only men seemingly capable of forming a threat to the drug lord. Tragically, in one of the most shocking turns of the season, Carrillo found himself betrayed just as it seemed he was on the cusp of bringing Escobar to heel in 'The Good, the Bad, and the Dead.' With Carrillo wounded by Escobar's men, Escobar revealed a souvenir that Carrillo had sent him as a warning—a bullet, intended for Pablo, sent by a courier to the drug lord: one that Escobar then used to execute the Search Bloc commander.

Producer Jesse Rose Moore said that the death of Carrillo was planned to be completely unexpected. "Bringing him back in season two and then almost immediately killing him off was meant to be shocking," Moore explained, noting that the character send-off also differentiated Carrillo from Search Bloc commander Hugo Martinez. "Martinez wasn't throwing people out of helicopters like Carrillo. Murphy always walks a pretty straight line—he's a cop, he believes in right and wrong, he's trying to be morally the way he should. Peña is a bit more gray—less black and white, and Carrillo, similarly, you have to do bad things sometimes to take down bad people." Carrillo represented a level of amorality that was illustrated in degrees with the show's leads.

BELOW: The aftermath of Escobar's ambush on Colonel Carrillo.

LOS PEPES

s the outrages of Escobar's reign of terror were felt among the civilian population and in the Colombian government, rivals to the Medellín cartel began to smell blood in the water. The result was the formation of a civilian vigilante force called Los Pepes, their name derived from an acronym for *Perseguidos por Pablo Escobar* (Persecuted by Pablo Escobar.) Los Pepes was created to bring justice to all the victims of Escobar's violence.

In reality, the alliance between the Cali cartel, the Castaños, and Moncada was based on fact. The Cali cartel used Los Pepes as a way to get rid of their rivals in an aim to control the market. In the series the mysterious Los Pepes was a creature born from the cash of the Cali cartel and Judy Moncada's long-nursed desire for vengeance against Escobar—a clever way of aligning these historical entities in dramatic form and allying them with DEA Agent Pena.

At one point Los Pepes was even accused of being organized and supported by Search Bloc itself. The group was able to operate outside the law, in effect using the narco terrorist tactics invented by Pablo Escobar against him. "Los Pepes was a joint venture between the Cali cartel, Judy Moncada, the Castaño brothers, and the Search Bloc as well," Andrés Baiz says. "Search Bloc was part of it 100%. It wasn't only Search Bloc but they were part of it, it was a joint effort."

"LOS PEPES WAS A JOINT VENTURE"

ANDRÉS BAIZ

ABOVE: A meeting between Escobar's enemies.

SE BUSCA

PABLO EMILIO ESCOBAR GAVIRIA

SOLICITADO POR LA JUSTICIA

A quien sumisistre información que permita
su captura, se le ofrece como recompensa

$ 2.700'000.000.oo

DOS MIL SETECIENTOSMILLONES DE PESOS.

| GONZALO RODRIGUEZ GACHA | JORGE LUIS OCHOA VÁSQUEZ | FABIO OCHOA VÁSQUEZ | GUSTAVO GAVIRIA |

| "LA QUICA" | "GALEANO" | "AREIZA" | "MECHAS" | "EL CHAMO" | "EL TIO" | "EL NEGRO" | "MONCADA" | "PITUFO" |

y por cada uno de estos prófugos la suma de

$ 100'000.000.oo

CIEN MILLONES DE PESOS

WARFARE AT A WEDDING

By expanding the *Narcos* world into the rich environment of Cali and its cartels, the show evolved its visual palette and illustrated the scope and complexity of the cartel world. While Escobar had allies in the Ochoas and Priscos, he also had enemies like the Cali cartel. The Cali godfathers moved gradually to the forefront over the course of three seasons, getting more scenes and developing as characters so that by the end of season two the audience understood their motivations. This built from the early confrontations between Escobar and Pacho in season one. Then in season two, the audience was introduced to Gilberto and Miguel Rodríguez, and Escobar was increasingly boxed in by Los Pepes. Feeling ever more desperate, he set his sights on the Cali cartel as the likely source behind this new assault on his power. The show's creative team dramatized Escobar lashing out at his enemy in a daring bombing, intended to kill Gilberto Rodriguez at his daughter's wedding. The explosives failed to kill the intended target, but the resulting panic (brilliantly staged by Josef Kubota Wladyka) made for one of the series' most vivid action sequences. The scene laid the groundwork for a harrowing retaliation from Los Pepes against Escobar and his family, and set the stage for the shift from the Medellín Cartel to the Cali cartel in season three.

ABOVE AND RIGHT: Photos from the set of the wedding.

BELOW: Concept design by Salvador Parra.

CHRISTMAS STREETS

The terrifying climax of Los Pepes' war against Pablo Escobar took place at Christmas time, when Pablo's mother Hermilda disobeyed her son's orders to stay in hiding to attend mass. This resulted in a violent raid on the house where Pablo and his family were staying. "Colombia and especially Medellín, they have a very strong idea of Christmas," production designer Salvador Parra said. "They get crazy with Christmas and they put lights everywhere so it's like something the people can't miss—even in the worst moments in Colombia, Medellín is full of life during Christmas. They really love that and we tried to get as close as we could to the craziness that people of Medellín have." Part of Parra's job was also to foreshadow the raid with some ugly warning signs for the Medellín cartel. "The story was about the killing at Christmas—there were all these Castaños and Cali cartel guys trying to kill the Medellín cartel guys. We had one scene where there was a little message for Pablo, where they just kill three guys in the middle of a square that is completely decorated for Christmas. We put one thing that was beautiful—there were little kids singing carols with candles. Then the camera moves to show these bodies that were killed in the plaza with all these Christmas decorations as an art installation. That was really interesting to design that and not be absurd. It was hard to integrate both things, the killings and the Christmas, but I think it works."

ABOVE RIGHT: Sketch and final image of the Christmas streets murders.

ABOVE AND BELOW: Concept designs by Salvador Parra.

THE CHRISTMAS RAID

Accomplished in one bravura shot, the terrifying nighttime raid on Escobar's compound showed, for the first time, the tide turning against Escobar and the very real stakes of life and death for the drug lord and his family in 'Los Pepes.' Carlo Bernard says the Christmas raid was an amalgamation of details from numerous attempts to take down Escobar at his various residences. "There were dozens of raids and there were raids certainly where the coffee on the table is still warm, so there were some very near misses. Of course as the Los Pepes aspect of it came into play it got even more complicated because they were also doing their own raids and we sort of combined some things in that. [Escobar's] mother's house was blown up, some extended family members were murdered by Los Pepes, so there was simultaneously a manhunt for him. But at the same time the Los Pepes had begun to target his family with the motive being to terrorize the terrorist and make him feel afraid, make him feel under pressure, which although morally dubious seems like it actually had its effect."

When Escobar's daughter, after being dragged through the night under gunfire to a safe house, worried that Santa Claus wouldn't be able to find them, the Christmas raid struck a note of pathos that made Escobar seem particularly vulnerable. "I remember reading an account of when Escobar was on the run and his family was ensconced in the Tacomiendo Hotel in the Los Pepes phase," Carlo Bernard says. "The family is being guarded by government that can barely stomach it, and these attacks are happening every day. There was an anecdote of the daughter playing by herself in the hallway of this hotel and singing this Christmas carol to herself about how Los Pepes was going to kill her father. And any time you see the story from her point of view, this six- or seven-year-old little girl who's living in a strange hotel with a bunch of government bodyguards who probably aren't too happy to be doing it, it's where it really becomes fascinating because there's sort of victims everywhere. Season two was really where the emotions in my opinion got really powerful, because that aspect of this guy's life, going from incredibly powerful man who could do whatever he wants to a guy whose world is getting smaller and smaller and who is separated from his family is really fascinating—the emotions are very Shakespearean and human. Even as the man is thought of as a monster the story itself is very ripe with emotion."

Cinematographer Luis David Sansans worked closely with director Josef Kubota Wladyka to choreograph the virtuoso camerawork that captured the raid. "We went to the location three or four times to set up the lighting and how we could make it happen. We started to create the choreography and how this was going to be, and we had between prep and shoot half a day for that shot. We recorded the choreography by ourselves without actors; we talked with the actors about it but they didn't know the location. Same for special effects—we did blocking with actors first, then we showed the crew, and we explained to the special effects people what we wanted to do—we told them we wanted to break windows and make it real, not try to depend on visual effects. We did 95% of the shot on location with real special effects. All the actors were really happy and very excited to do these kind of shots because that involves everybody, and that gets everybody excited and happy to do a challenge like this."

Part of the sequence's shock value came from setting up the driver who had taken Hermilda to mass as the POV for the raid—until he was unexpectedly killed halfway through the sequence. Sansans credits director Josef Kubota Wladyka with that idea. "We said, 'After we come out from the house, what's gonna happen?' Because nothing is happening from there ○ to the inside of the house again, so he came up with that idea of the driver that started the whole situation because he took Escobar's mother to church. That was the perfect time to close that character and say, 'You made a mistake and you pay for it.' I think the idea from Josef that was really clever was to not see the enemy. Everything is sound design and you just see the muzzle flashes in the deep background but you don't see faces, you don't see anybody, which creates more tension. It tells you that they're surrounded and they don't know where they're coming from, and the mess is inside the house and with the characters. Second unit shot guys shooting between the trees just in case we needed intercuts, but when they saw the sequence the producers thought it worked pretty well and they decided to leave it as it was. That's the first time that Pablo is under attack directly. He was under a menace the whole time but that's really the first time he's in real danger, where the enemy really gets into his life, himself and his family, and that's why we wanted to do something different for that special moment."

ABOVE: The first gunshots are heard.
BELOW: Escobar defends his family from the attack.

PROFILE:
HERMILDA GAVIRIA

P ablo Escobar's willful mother was fiercely loyal to her son. "We had this great Chilean actress, Paulina García," Chris Brancato says. "Pablo's mother was a school teacher but right along for the ride, so we had her in the pilot sewing linings into his coat so that a guy can smuggle cocaine to the U.S. She was just a fun mom with a larcenous streak."

Hermilda was always willing to break the rules for the sake of her son. While the family was in hiding, she told a story to Tata: a young, bullied Pablo needed shoes and a penniless Hermilda stole him a pair from the store. The tale gives the impression of a loving,

protective mother but Hermilda's moral of the story was, "Being poor is not an excuse to look like you are," putting the ideals of money and status above the law.

She was resolved to stand by her son, even through the atrocities he commited and caused. Chris Brancato remembers one of his favorite scenes with the headstrong mother, "After Gustavo dies, and Pablo comes back home and his mother comes and comforts him. That was really cool and the director shot it in one shot and it's a very effective scene." The character paints a portrait of a woman who is perhaps her son's enabler, but also loved him unconditionally.

PROFILE:
TATA ESCOBAR

Tata Escobar (Paulina Gaitán) was the strong and determined wife of one of the world's most notorious men. While Pablo Escobar's regard for his family was well documented, the details regarding his wife and children often had to be dramatized. "The reality of trying to do the show is you're obviously not privy to familial conversations, you're not privy to anything apart from DEA wiretaps, but we wanted to make there be a kind of epic love between these two people," Chris Brancato says. "We wanted her to kind of have this willful ignorance about the level of her husband's violence and psychopathology, and I just think Paulina Gaitán was really perfect for that role. You really sort of like the two of them together."

Tata remained loyal to Pablo, ignoring his affairs, enduring multiple assaults on her family homes, and standing by him through his exile—all for the love of her husband, and to keep her family protected. One of Tata's most memorable scenes was when, in attempting to keep her family safe, she accepted a visit from her husband's mistress, Valeria. Tata Escobar had a composure that remained even after the death of her husband, when she was able to reach an understanding with the fearsome Gilberto Rodríguez, so that her children would be safe.

THE ESCOBARS' ATTEMPT AT ASYLUM

In an illustration of Steve Murphy's dogged determination to keep up the pressure on Escobar, the DEA agent followed Escobar's wife and children to Germany. This was in plain sight of the Escobar clan who had no idea who he was. He ensured that customs agents in Germany had all the information they needed to prevent the exhausted Escobars from being able to remain in Europe, which forced them to return to Colombia where they could remain pawns in the government's ongoing campaign against Pablo.

Producer Jesse Rose Moore said that Murphy's pursuit of Escobar's family also showed a diversion between his character and Peña: "At that point you start to have Murphy and Peña taking slightly different tracks. Earlier on they're more of a team, the way [DEA agents] Feistl and Van Ness are in season three. But as season two goes on and Peña is getting more involved in

Los Pepes, Murphy's following a slightly different path and not knowing exactly what his partner is involved in. Murphy's story is following more the human side—he sees the family, he feels bad for Tata, he feels bad for the kids, because even though he knows Pablo is a monster, it's also affecting the kids and affecting more lives than he previously thought about." Moore recalled that the DEA agents discussed the toll the attacks on Escobar by Los Pepes had taken on Pablo's young daughter, who had suffered hearing loss from being around gunfire and grenade explosions during some of the assaults. "She did go deaf in one ear. I'm trying to remember if it was Murphy or Peña but one of them told me that they saw the daughter at the airport one time when they were trying to get away. She was just sitting there playing with her dog and she looked just lost, just a sad little girl and you really felt sorry for her."

ABOVE: A concept design of Frankfurt Airport by Salvador Parra.

ABOVE AND BELOW: Murphy keeps his eye on Tata.

ABOVE: A worried Tata makes a phonecall.

STREET BOMB

ABOVE: The model building created by the production design team.

ABOVE: The devastating effect of Escobar's wrath.

Escobar's violent affect on life in Medellín and Bogotá was graphically illustrated by a thoughtless street bombing that mowed down dozens of innocents. Recreating this historic incident presented Salvador Parra with the opportunity to match news photographs and video of the real event, and employ a time-honored, old-style special effect technique. "One of the reasons I accepted this job was to create really shocking images of all the terror that came out of the bombings of Pablo in Bogotá and in Medellín," Parra said. "The bombing scene we created really happened: it was a bomb that Pablo put in Bogotá downtown, close to the library." While the production worked to recreate the real-life location as authentically as possible, practical considerations meant that Parra and his crew had to relocate from downtown, where the original blast occurred. "It was crazy there and you have traffic and we were exploding a bomb, so it was not production-friendly in many ways," Parra said. "We picked another part of the downtown that was better but those buildings were not exactly the same ones in terms of architecture and structure and size, so we decided to create a little model like a miniature you would

shoot in-camera during the 1940s." Parra used the miniature to recreate the real-life building exterior seen in photos and rigged the model to explode, shooting the small-scale blast at high speed to enhance its scale and then compositing it into the filmed location. "What you can see is the street, the people, the vendors, extras walking, and suddenly a huge explosion happening, and it really fools the frame—it's super scary, and you can see the aftermath," Parra said. "And what was really beautiful about it was we looked at a lot of the real-life footage from that scene because we wanted to blend it with the archival footage, so it really mimics perfectly, because the buildings are exactly the same. Because we used a miniature, we were able to use exactly the same street minutes before the explosion and then for the aftermath, which was people without arms and a whole inferno there. That was one of the biggest challenges in terms of design and how to do it in one single day, because you don't have so much time to do these perfect pieces. So in the same day we shot the book store like the people were just buying books, then the explosion and then the aftermath full of police and the fire department."

TOP: A concept design of the street and shops before the bomb.

LEFT AND ABOVE: The car bomb that killed dozens of people.

A FAMILY REUNION

s Escobar, all but stripped of his wealth and power, remained on the run, communicating with his family only intermittently by radio phone, he retreated to his father's farm and had to confront his father's contempt for the life he had chosen. Sticking by Escobar's side was Limón—seemingly the last loyal member of Escobar's once-great army of narcos. Carlo Bernard says that the showrunner and creative team extrapolated on what they knew about Escobar's father Abel (played by Alfredo Castro). "[Pablo] had a father, but there was a little bit of a blank canvas of what were those last few months like. We knew he was on the run, we knew that it was essentially him and Limón as he lost ally after ally and Los Pepes were slowly but surely putting him into a corner, so for us it was a question of, we don't know what he did, but what if it was something like this? The thrust of that was more imagining what might have happened or what could have happened at that time."

Cinematographer Luis David Sansans took a pastoral approach to shooting the farmhouse scenes, bringing an intimate focus to these final weeks in Escobar's once-tyrannical life. "For all that period of time, we thought that it was going to be a good idea to make it more aesthetic, the composition more creative, because this is like a hiatus between all the bad period of time that he's experiencing at that point in his life," Sansans says. "What we thought about this reencounter between the father and Pablo was he was going to ask for forgiveness in his

life, and to come back to this relationship with his father which didn't happen during these years because he was a narco and a killer and his father was in another perspective about life. So everything is very static, very contemplative, and at some point Pablo realizes that that's not going to happen—that his father hates him because of what he did, and he has to have a confrontation because his father is not being honest with him and he wants to confront him."

The confrontation itself comes in the form of the slaughter of a pig—a bloody reminder of Pablo's years of killing. When Abel coldly orders Pablo to slit the dead pig open, the shocked Pablo winds up doused in blood, and Abel taunts his son over his squeamishness. "Killing that pig, having blood spraying everywhere and mostly on Pablo, and you have some kind of déjà vu of Pablo in season one when he kills one of his partners in *La Catedral*, when he starts killing these guys with a pool cue and he's covered with blood. So it was a kind of homage of what he is in reality—he is a killer and he is a bad guy and he will have blood on his hands until the last day of his life. I think it's a confrontation between father and son, which should be very painful. It was very simple—just having these two great actors and this situation of confrontation and human behavior and the location was great—the element of the pig added drama to the scene, and at the end, it reflected what the character of Pablo Escobar was."

ABEL'S FARM

For 'Nuestra Finca,' Salvador Parra had to find a location that conceivably represented the home where Pablo grew up as a young child, where his father still lived the same life that Pablo fled from. "That was something the director Andrés Baiz wanted: a very Colombian type of house for a very old man with all his morals," Parra said. "We found a house in a beautiful land full of cows, but they have a contemporary type of architecture. It didn't look like an old house from the 20s—I wanted the idea that the family had lived there for many years, so we took a new house and added more plaster to the walls, and we put a lot of patina on it and destroyed a little bit of the walls so they looked like they had

been made in adobe." Parra wanted the house to reflect Abel's simplicity in contrast to the morally compromised life led by his son. "That was the intention of his house, to make the story of Abel in those walls and also in the furniture—a very simple house with two beds and a wooden table, very humble, mostly a shack. But we wanted that feeling like this guy was a farmer who wakes up at seven in the morning and gets to bed at six or seven and lives the way he wants to be, which is a contradiction with Pablo, because Pablo's a guy who cannot wait a second, he wants to do something—with Abel it's like eternal life, he could live 100 or 200 years and be the same guy."

ABOVE AND RIGHT: Final photos from the set of the farm.

BELOW AND RIGHT: Concept designs by Salvador Parra.

L'S FARM HOUSE

ESCOBAR'S LAST REVERIE

One final day a lonely and haunted Escobar took a walk near a park. The nearby police officers ignored him, unaware that the state's most notorious fugitive was standing right before them. Lost in a reverie of unaccustomed freedom, Pablo wandered among his people, mixing with them freely with no fear of pursuit. He finally relaxed on a park bench where he reunited with his cousin Gustavo—a ghost vision encountered in this hallucinogenic, pre-death moment. Eric Newman says that director Andrés Baiz dictated the approach. "Andrés said, 'I want to do something surreal here, and it's beautiful.'"

"We shot that in Medellín and all the people around are real people we hired in the moment so it was very authentic," Baiz adds. "It's a very emotional moment and I have to say that Wagner Moura and I worked really well together and we didn't follow the script 100%. We had many opportunities before we shot to rewrite scenes and we told the writers what we were going to do. That scene we rewrote completely and the scenes at Pablo's father's farm we kind of went out on our own. Sometimes we just went and took the camera and said, 'Let's just have you smoking a joint in the middle of all these flowers and maybe they'll put it in the cut,' and 90% of the time that we did that it went into the cut. We improvised and had the freedom of doing things in the moment because of Wagner and my relationship with him."

Wagner Moura cites Escobar's reverie in the park just before his death as his favorite scene in the series. "It was beautiful to see my brother Juan Pablo Raba, with whom I started this journey, back there to finalize it. We both got very emotional

ABOVE: Escobar is reunited with his trusted partner, Gustavo, in a brief moment of respite.

"GUSTAVO WAS THERE AS PABLO'S CONSCIENCE TO REASSURE HIM OF HIS REAL NATURE"

WAGNER MOURA

in that scene. Gustavo was there as Pablo's conscience to reassure him of his real nature. I love that scene."

Cinematographer Luis David Sansans executed the look of the park sequence. "We were thinking what should we do there—shall we change visually something, make it softer in contrast or create a dream sequence? And at the end we played like if it was normal life. Like it was part of that moment in Escobar's life—something happens and to make it believable to the audience that he was in that world, he survived in a certain way. Because he [Gustavo] survived in his mind, in Escobar's mind. He was in a need of someone to talk to, someone in which Escobar trusts his life, and with whom he made deals and with whom he made his empire—he was his right hand, his brother, his family, his confidante, so I think it was a good idea not to create something else around the scene, but just them. And the only thing we played is the old guy, the old man that sits with

Escobar, in a certain moment that old man becomes when you call to Pablo and come back, it's not the old man anymore, it's Gustavo."

Sansans used a Steadicam to create a feeling of calm as Escobar walks through the park among his people. "He had a joint, it's his birthday, and he just decides to enjoy life for the last time and to visit his town, to visit Medellín, to walk around his streets and be around his people. So having that moment with him in the middle of the park surrounded by kids, old men, families having fun, enjoying and showing to the audience that in this circular movement where sometimes the focus was on the background to see what he was looking at like some kind of POV but involved in the character himself on the shot. I think that connects you with the human side of Pablo. I think that was the idea of having that shot on Steadicam—to show the audience that he was going through a peaceful moment before he dies."

PROFILE:
GUSTAVO GAVIRIA

Pablo Escobar's cousin and childhood friend, Gustavo hooked Escobar up with the chemist "Cockroach" and subsequently the cocaine trade and became Escobar's most trusted lieutenant—and in a way his conscience—in the Medellín cartel. The only one who was able to speak with complete honesty to Escobar, Gustavo disapproved of Escobar's political ambitions and often called him out on his violent excesses.

"That is the incredible actor Juan Pablo Raba, and those guys, when we cast Gustavo Gaviria, Carla Hool, our other casting director, suggested Juan Pablo," Chris Brancato says. "Wagner's in Medellín studying Spanish, and Juan Pablo is from Colombia, one of the nicest guys in the world, and they took a drive together to Hacienda Nápoles, what remains of Pablo's estate. It was a seven or eight-hour drive and they totally bonded, so from the very moment we were down there starting to shoot they had this connection to one another, and to me Gustavo is one of my favorite characters."

Although Gustavo sometimes acted as a steadying hand to his cousin, he wasn't devoid of violent acts—his willingness to complete violent orders on behalf of Escobar ended in Gustavo making quite a few enemies of his own. And unfortunately Gustavo's honesty didn't extend to his own sexual relationship with the sister of one of the Ochoa brothers, which he concealed from Escobar. The affair with Marina Ochoa forced her brothers to tip Carrillo off about Gustavo's whereabouts in order to separate him from their sister. This led to Gustavo's capture, beating, interrogation, and death at the hands of Colonel Carrillo and his men—many of whom were eager to enact their own vengeance on the narco. Gustavo nevertheless endured Carrillo's torture bravely and refused to inform on Escobar.

BELOW: Escobar, Gustavo, and Poison on one the smuggling routes.

PROFILE:
HUGO MARTINEZ

Although Colonel Carrillo was effective in his mission to bring the Medellín cartel down, his methods included violence, torture, and murder, and showrunner Eric Newman didn't want the morally compromised character to be the one to catch Escobar. Horacio Carrillo's death paved the way for the introduction of a new character to lead the Search Bloc against Escobar. Colonel Hugo Martinez was a real-life figure who had cooperated with the production in its creation, and he provided the show with a real-life Colombian hero, so the creative team decided to introduce him as the character to end the reign of Escobar. In contrast to his predecessor, Col. Hugo Martinez (Juan Pablo Shuk) was determined to work within the law in his pursuit of the Colombian drug lords. He was a quiet and dogged adversary for Escobar in the Colombian government. His methodical pursuit of Pablo Escobar—with the help of his son Hugo Martinez Jr.—helped lead to Escobar's capture and death.

PROFILE:
HUGO MARTINEZ JR.

Humiliated by cartel drug runners at a traffic checkpoint in 'The Enemies of My Enemy', young military officer Hugo Martinez Jr. (Sebastián Vega) was determined to atone for being a public embarrassment to his father and became an expert in sonic surveillance. He eventually helped to track down Pablo Escobar, leading to Escobar's final capture and death.

The involvement of Hugo Martinez Jr. is one of the most dramatically effective elements of the show's end game for season two—one of the aspects of the show that seems so perfect that viewers might understandably believe it was invented for the series. But it's actually true to life. "Martinez, the guy who led Search Bloc, his son was a radio technician and that's all true," Carlo Bernard explains. "The kid had developed this radio triangulation technique and it's literally too crazy to make up—Hugo Martinez Jr. was a real kid and he was the one

who saw Pablo on the phone. That last day is a pretty accurate depiction, episode 210. The broad strokes of the events are that Martinez was driving around trying to track this signal as Escobar was on the phone with his family. Part of the tragedy was that Escobar was for a long time pretty disciplined about getting off the phone quickly to avoid being captured. But the longer he was on the run, the more he was missing his family,

his discipline started to slip and he was on the phone too long, and that allowed Martinez Jr. to catch a signal. He was actually driving down the street when he saw Escobar on the phone and realized, 'Holy shit, I just saw Pablo Escobar.' And they pulled over and made the phone call and he sort of had to stay put there as the other troops moved in even though he wasn't on the armed response side of things. But the kid had staked out the place to make sure Escobar didn't take off as the cops were closing in."

The one invented part of the story was Martinez Jr.'s humiliation at the hands of Escobar's men in the casual flouting of a street checkpoint. "There had been a couple of notorious failures that had been pretty embarrassing and one in particular that the son was involved in," Bernard says. "A couple of high profile humiliating raids, one at a church where they'd torn the place up and nobody was there, so the kid was convinced that this equipment was the answer and there was a lot of skepticism within the other parts of the police towards the equipment. So there was definitely a little of the son trying to redeem himself and prove that this technology works and if you use it right this will help to catch him, and in the end, it was. The truth is pretty hard to top."

PABLO'S FINAL HOURS

Throughout season two, production designer Salvador Parra used the sets to illustrate Escobar's journey from kingpin to hunted fugitive. "We start with a beautiful *finca* and he's running and escaping to another and another, and every time he escapes the *finca* becomes more crappy, more humble, with more corruption and run-down," This design motif continued up till Pablo's final hideout, where he was lying low in a small house without money, without his *sicarios*, with just one follower, Limón. "We wanted to do this progression from nice *fincas* to ones that are collapsing to finally this dark hole he's in when he dies."

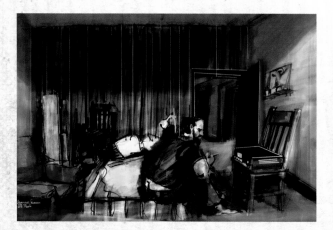 

ABOVE: Final photo and concept designs of Escobar's hideout.

THE END OF PABLO

Routed from the cheap suburban apartment he had shared with Limón, Escobar fled desperately across the rooftops of the surrounding buildings pursued by DEA agent Murphy and Colombian troops. After years of holding Colombia itself under his foot, Pablo Escobar died in an ignominious, short rooftop pursuit.

Most audience members know that Escobar dies, and they might know where he died but not the exact circumstances. Although there have been some wild rumors surrounding his death, the creative team decided to follow what they believed to be the most probable: that the Search Bloc accomplished their mission.

Showrunner Eric Newman strived to present the most accurate possible recreation of this historic moment, but while the actual building still existed, it had been renovated and the rooftop where the final shootout took place had been built over. Fortunately, a rooftop identical to the one on which Escobar died was available at the house next door and the production was able to secure this location for the sequence.

The heart-stopping climax to *Narcos'* first two seasons and Escobar's story, Pablo's death sequence was an opportunity to show the Colombian officers driving the raid and the DEA in a supporting role. Murphy, the American POV, was a participant, but not the bringer of Escobar's fate, and the *Narcos'* creative team used the occasion to showcase the courage and dedication of the Colombian people in the fight against narco-terrorism.

Luis Sansans says there was some thought to shooting the death pursuit in a single camera shot in the same way that the Christmas raid by Los Pepes on Escobar's compound had been filmed. Ultimately it was decided to shoot with multiple cameras to capture some vital details. "Since there are only two or three characters it was going to be difficult to engage all of them. But once they jump out of the window, it's just [Pablo] running because Limón dies at that point. We decided to roll the full sequence in one shot until the moment Pablo dies, because then it's a shock—it's like, 'What happened? What's gonna happen now?'"

To build more tension for this momentous scene, the team decided to film part of the chase sequence with a handheld camera. When Pablo died, the filming changed back from the handheld camera to provide a peaceful shot. "Even the exact moment where he dies, when he gets shot, it becomes static. Like if something happened and time stopped in the world," says Luis Sansans.

ABOVE: Just moments after the shot that killed Escobar.

THE RISE OF A NEW EMPIRE

The gen of Cali

war on drugs.
Unfortunately, the Cali
Cartel was already
working its ki
strategy

El Ajedrecista and El Señor

ation fails

to
Colombian and
governments to se
time. These
members will be

CALI

In the minds of everyone involved, *Narcos* was always bigger than Escobar, so the idea of expanding the storyline and introducing other cartels was there before shooting began on the first season.

While working on season two, the creative team began to plant the seeds for the Cali cartel. "That was the idea, to get the Cali characters started and up on their feet so that they could be prominent in the third season after Escobar dies. That's why the end of episode ten ends with Gilberto toasting, because they were really behind Escobar's demise— they funded Los Pepes and they fueled all the antagonism against him in back channels in very, very smart ways. So the idea was the demise of Pablo yields the rise of the Cali cartel, and also from the DEA side, you cut off the head of the snake and another head grows back. And all the energy and effort and the compromises Peña made and the suffering Murphy goes through

doesn't mean much, because Cali rises from the ashes of Pablo, and it's just this feeling these guys have of running in sand."

As Escobar was weakened, the Cali cartel grew in power, yet Cali leader Gilberto Rodríguez was determined to avoid Escobar's inevitable fate by making his own grand bargain with the Colombian government. "In a lot of ways Cali really is a response to Escobar," Carlo Bernard says about the rise of the Cali cartel beginning in season two, which laid the foundation for the third season. "There were things done by the Colombian government and the American government, compromises made to take out Escobar that helped to empower the Cali cartel. In some ways that helped to strengthen the hand of corruption, because Escobar was so famous that there was a sense of, 'do whatever it takes to take him down.' In that sort of vacuum of moral clarity, the Cali cartel sprang into power. So that was also part of the story for season three—it's about some of the compromises of the hunt for Escobar coming home to roost and the transgressions and shortcuts of the past have come back to haunt them a bit in season three."

With the inspiration for season three coming from the experiences of Jorge Salcedo, the first episode, 'The Kingpin Strategy' kicked off by introducing the main subject. "To me that was one of the show's most critical episodes," Bernard says. "After Escobar died in the season finale of season two I think a lot of people rightly said, 'What do they do now?' Wagner Moura was in the midst of providing one of the great performances in the history of TV and they killed him off. I think there was a pretty high degree of skepticism that the show could survive without Escobar, so that was why that first episode of season three introduces Salcedo. There's Peña's desire for redemption, and Jorge Salcedo's desire to start a new life and Gilberto's desire to step away, and you know that none of these guys are going to get what they want."

For Bernard, shifting the focus to a more ordinary man like Salcedo as opposed to an epic figure like Escobar created a powerful way to bring audiences into the story. "There's a lot of family stuff between Miguel and Gilberto, because Miguel is really the silent partner and his brother is really the leader. And then Miguel gets a chance to step out into the spotlight and we see what that means to him emotionally—and the father/son dynamics between Miguel and Salcedo, and Miguel and his own son." Bernard explained that the third season shifts the perspective on the downfall of a cartel to someone in "middle management" as opposed to a frighteningly powerful figure like Pablo Escobar. " In Salcedo, you're taking someone who's recognizable and not too different from us at the center of the story as he was in real life. What was exciting about it is there's no way you were going to be able to top Escobar as a straight-up antihero villain, because the truth is too crazy to top. But by taking a different dramatic point of view and telling it from the point of view of a guy who's stuck in the trap he's put himself in and is trying to get out, that gave us a different genre and point of view to play the story from."

PROFILE:
CHRIS FEISTL

Chris Feistl (Michael Stahl-David) was based on the real-life DEA agent (and Narcos consultant), who was one of the key contacts with Cali cartel head of security Jorge Salcedo, the informant who would help the DEA and the Colombian government bring down the cartel. Along with Daniel Van Ness, Feistl was instrumental in grooming Salcedo as an informant. The challenge of balancing Salcedo's concerns for his family and his own safety against the need to get intel on the Cartel formed the basis of much of the third season's unique suspense.

Director Andrés Baiz says that Feistl and Van Ness had to operate somewhat in the shadow of Peña but still shepherded the critical involvement of Jorge Salcedo. "It was hard because they're really not replacing Peña and Murphy because Peña is still the lead in terms of the DEA, but [Feistl and Van Ness] had the groundwork, the action sequences and the tension. We actually shot a lot of their scenes in Cali because Peña had to stay in Bogotá because he was DEA [Country Attaché] at the time."

Baiz says that the DEA agents first had to decide whether Salcedo was trustworthy, and whether protecting him should take precedence over nailing Miguel Rodríguez.

"All their dilemmas floated around this idea of the snitch or the informant, and the ethical or moral questions that come into play when you have to defend a person that you don't know is good or bad, whether he's lying or telling the truth, or whether he's a coward or being brave. That's mainly what the characters revolved around."

Early in the season, Chris Feistl was a foil to Peña, who was burnt out and jaded after the moral compromises he witnessed and took part in. In many ways, Chris was a catalyst for the DEA in season three as he challenged and invigorated Peña with his zealous spirit and strong work ethic. Actor Michael Stahl David extensively researched his role and met and conversed with the real Chris Feistl multiple times to get background and a feel for the character. Producer Jesse Rose Moore was involved in casting Stahl-David as Feistl. "We wanted someone who didn't look too far off from the real Feistl and we were also looking for someone who would be able to handle dialogue in Spanish. What was great about Michael was he had grown up going to a bilingual school so he's actually pretty fluent in Spanish. That's always one of the challenges that we have is finding people who are bilingual. The real Feistl also had a bit of a mullet so we gave Michael a little bit of a mullet in back."

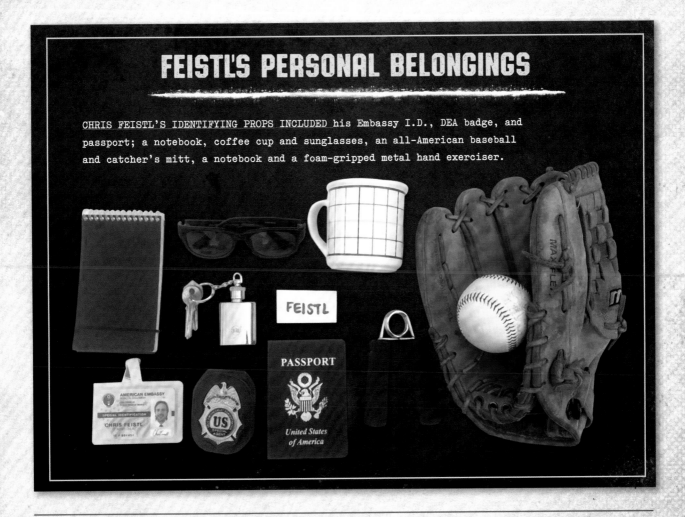

FEISTL'S PERSONAL BELONGINGS

CHRIS FEISTL'S IDENTIFYING PROPS INCLUDED his Embassy I.D., DEA badge, and passport; a notebook, coffee cup and sunglasses, an all-American baseball and catcher's mitt, a notebook and a foam-gripped metal hand exerciser.

PROFILE:
DANIEL VAN NESS

An American DEA agent partnered with Chris Feistl during the 1990s, Van Ness (Matt Whelan) had previously served in Chile. The two were then assigned to Cali, Colombia, and often worked with less-than-upstanding police officers in order to gain an advantage on the cartel. Van Ness and Feistl worked with Cali cartel security chief Jorge Salcedo to get strategic intelligence on the Cali network and worked under Javier Peña in operations against the cartel. Although inspired by DEA agent Chris Feistl's real-life partner, Van Ness's name was altered for the TV series. "Those were based on real guys, Chris Feistl and his partner, who were great and who were the guys who were in Cali and worked with Salcedo and they were really Salcedo's handlers," Carlo Bernard explains. "They were instrumental in taking down the Cali cartel. Chris had retired and was able to help us and was a fantastic consultant."

The characterization of Feistl and Van Ness differed from Murphy and Peña—because Peña's redemption was the big dramatic DEA character arc of the season, Feistl and Van Ness were written with less of a personal vendetta and more professional focus. The drama in their story came from their relationship with Salcedo—some of the partners' most memorable scenes were the tense interactions they had as handlers.

In talking with the real Chris Feistl, the creative team found that Jorge Salcedo was very important to the DEA partners. Van Ness and Feistl were aware of the risks to their informant and his family, and as a result of that, they worried for his safety. It was a difficult relationship as, though the agents wanted to protect him, they couldn't guarantee his safety because of the dangerous circumstances.

DEA SAFEHOUSE

Similar to his designs of the other sets, Salvador Parra ensured that the DEA safe house would tie into a real-life story from the war on drugs. "The DEA safe house was a hard place to do because once again we have to put some history into that little house in Cali. This house was supposed to be owned by the CIA when Noriega was in Panama, so there was a lot of research about Noriega when our DEA guys arrive at that house." The Panamanian dictator was involved in the drug trade in the 80s so the crossover for DEA investigations into Manuel Noriega would fit the timing for the Cali Cartel. "All that information gives you the period and the year where you are and the important characters that were also involved with the cartel like Noriega."

THIS SPREAD: Concept designs by Salvador Parra.

EXT SAFE HOUSE
NARCOS 3 / PARRA 2017

SAFE HOUSE CALI

PEÑA'S PROMOTION

The series' creative team made the decision to transfer the focus to the Cali cartel and retain the presence and perspective of Peña as opposed to introducing entirely new villains and protagonists for season three. "At the time it was a pretty audacious and somewhat nerve-inducing idea just because Wagner Moura was so powerful and Escobar was so hard to top," Bernard said, "so the decision was made to have Peña stay and perform some of the real-life actions that the agents did but to personify them for dramatic purposes through Peña."

Doug Miro says that by pitting Peña against the Cali cartel in season three, the show raised the dramatic stakes for the character. "On the narco side it's like one kingpin disappears and another kingpin rises, and they're all aggressive and ambitious and have knives out for each other. On the DEA side they feel like they're running in sand because of that, because we take out one and another comes in. That set up season three where now Peña, feeling like he compromised himself to get Pablo, wants some sense of redemption by going after the guy that blows up in Pablo's place. And the question is whether

"ONE KINGPIN DISAPPEARS AND ANOTHER KINGPIN RISES"

DOUG MIRO

he can get that redemption or whether it's even possible in this dark and gray world that he almost created himself, because he, in helping Los Pepes, facilitates Cali's rise."

Peña's presence throughout season three served the show's creative narrative but was a major dramatization of the historical record and one of the only significant departures from real life. The involvement of Chris Feistl and Daniel Van Ness adhered close to their actions in reality, but Peña and Murphy had both left Colombia shortly after the death of Escobar. Consequently Peña's character in these two seasons combines aspects of several other real-life officials who worked in Colombia at the time.

ABOVE RIGHT: A concept by Salvador Parra for Peña's new office.
BELOW: Giving press conferences was one responsibility of his promotion.

PROFILE:
GILBERTO RODRÍGUEZ

Known as "The Chess Player," Gilberto Rodríguez Orejuela was the leader, along with his brother Miguel, Chepe Santacruz Londoño, and Pacho Herrera, of the Cali cartel from the 1970s. He obscured the cartel's drug operations by investing their spoils in legitimate businesses and avoided the confrontational and violent excesses of the Medellín cartel, earning the cartel a nickname, "The Gentlemen of Cali." Gilberto methodically planned for his operation's long-term growth and stability, generating billions of dollars in profits each year.

Unlike Pablo Escobar, whose public reign of terror in Colombia received breathless media coverage and resulted in a wealth of available news footage, the Cali cartel members were far more secretive and private. This made it much harder to find video and photographs of the men to incorporate into the series. However, enough outlandish details about the Rodríguez brothers came to light during the research process to inform the portrayal of Gilberto and Miguel—the fact that Gilberto had multiple wives, and deemed himself an art collector and connoisseur, helped flesh out his portrayal in the series.

After the downfall of Escobar, the Cali cartel had a virtual monopoly on the cocaine trade, but also fell under increasing scrutiny by the authorities. This led Gilberto to concoct a "grand bargain" in which he and the Cali leaders would surrender and endure minimal jail time while preserving their drug profits. Played by popular Mexican actor Damián Alcázar, Gilberto Rodríguez appeared to be the logical leading character of season three as the mastermind behind the Cali cartel and its daring exit strategy. Instead, Gilberto was sidelined in prison from early in the season. "That was the design," says executive producer Carlo Bernard. "We've obviously seen these stories before and again it happened in real life, so we took that and kind of serviced it so it would be a big surprise. We start off clearly signaling Gilberto as sort of the guy, and he's obviously replacing Escobar, and then he gets arrested. The hope is that that's a big surprise, and then of course we tell the story dramatically from Miguel's point of view of him having to sit in the chair and become the leader of the cartel. It's a bit of a set angle to play, because you play it from the traverse point of view as the DEA and Colombians are closing in and doing their thing. It gives you a chance to play the human story of what it's like for someone who's been living in their brother's shadow and is leading the cartel for the first time to providing a surprise for the audience that is probably sitting back and assuming that Gilberto will get arrested in the last episode of the season."

"HE'S OBVIOUSLY REPLACING ESCOBAR, AND THEN HE GETS ARRESTED"

CARLO BERNARD

THIS SPREAD: Gilberto was a man of style.

PROFILE:
JORGE SALCEDO

In addition to forming one of the most riveting suspense storylines in the *Narcos* series, the story of Jorge Salcedo also allowed for one of the show's greatest ironies: that the downfall of the secretive and security-minded Cali cartel came about due to the betrayal by their own head of security. Once Miguel Rodríguez turned down Salcedo's resignation, Salcedo's position in the cartel became a ticking time bomb certain to end either in Salcedo's murder or in the exposure of the Cali cartel' top leaders.

Actor Matias Varela was excited to join the show after watching the first two seasons. "When I spoke to Eric he told me, 'I'm going to bestow a serious responsibility on your shoulders—this is a very important part on the show and to an extent he's actually the lead,' and I thought *yeah, right*. It didn't really dawn on me until I was about to do episode four or five—I started seeing okay, this is a lot of scenes, there's a lot of pages here and I'm working all the time. It took me a while to realize it was such a big part."

Varela didn't have access to the real Jorge Salcedo. "That said, I talked to a lot of the DEA people, especially Feistl, who was really approachable in a big way. So we spoke and then I read as much as I could find on the internet."

Varela also worked to create a background for the character that would explain how he got involved with the Cali cartel. "It was a lot of work to figure out who he was outside of the cartel—why did he get into it? I spent a good two months in preparing the background for him to figure out what kind of person he was to exist in a world that in all honesty wasn't really him. I would expect a very large percentage of the audience having an easier time relating to someone like Salcedo because he's a truly normal person. He loves his family, he puts his daughters to bed and reads bedtime stories to them, approachable stuff in comparison to shooting people and snorting cocaine. So Salcedo to an extent is the normal guy in the story and we see this world through his eyes, and I thought it was a great opportunity to do a part like that who was not the archetypical cartel member."

Doug Miro found Salcedo's character to be a key part of the third season's success, "He was so instrumental, he took so many risks, he had so much on the line and he was so high up in the cartel. There just aren't that many examples of that kind of story. So we were lucky—we were lucky it came through in Matias' performance, capturing the sympathetic family man and the guy who agreed to work for the cartel in the first place."

"HE WAS SO INSTRUMENTAL, HE TOOK SO MANY RISKS"

DOUG MIRO

LEFT: Salcedo's actions caused the death of his partner.

Miro saw a dichotomy in Salcedo that he found similar in a way to Pablo Escobar. "[Salcedo's] more of a victim but there's also a little bit of darkness in him, and he's also working for more redemption than Pablo ever was. A lot of the tension of the season is both him trying to save himself and his family, but also trying to find some redemption and literally save his own soul. That's the part I'm not sure he accomplishes. He saves his family but I'm not sure he feels like he saves his own soul from being part of the cartel."

Varela took some unusual strategies in reinforcing the character and his outlook. "Whenever he leaves his house he's always checking this gate for no apparent reason; he's always probing this gate with his hand, almost like it's a fixation or a tick or something, and he does that relentlessly every time he leaves the house." The cartel's surveillance operation covered the whole of the city and the team used creative camera work to give the viewer the impression that somebody was always watching—a key element in creating tensions within the season. Varela also worked on expanding that tension into his portrayal of Salcedo. "In a conversation with one of the directors we talked about what to do to create that sense of not being safe ever, not even in his own house: he never feels safe. To help me give that notion that, 'I might wind up dead right now if I leave the house,' I finally figured out I needed to put a rock in one of my shoes to get that feeling of being uncomfortable. That trick emphasized that fear and constant stress of not knowing what I have to do in the next minute or next hour."

Salcedo also indirectly, but consciously, causes the death of others, including his boss in the cartel Cordova, as the noose begins to tighten late in the season. "One of the scenes that was hard to do was when they kill my best friend and they kill the police captain and they make it sound like it's my fault, like it's Salcedo's fault, and I'm standing there thinking 'How can this be my fault?' Then I ask about it and they say, 'Congratulations, you just got a new job—I'm promoting you to that dead guy's job!' He's just witnessed the execution of his best friend and his best friend's wife, and the reason why they do it is Salcedo lies to get himself in the clear—he ends up in the clear but winds up killing his best friend and gets promoted on top of his best friend's death." For Varela, this pivotal moment leads to the death of Enrique. "That changes him and he goes into this darker phase and he ends up killing

ABOVE: A tense moment between Salcedo and his DEA handlers.

Enrique who is his close assistant—when he puts that pager in his pocket, that's a death sentence. Salcedo hands down is involved in the death of two of his closest friends and one of their wives and also Navegante, so clearly he's a complex guy. The question is, is it really okay to do what he did to save his own family? Because he destroyed families along the way. I suspect that most of us would do whatever it takes to save our own children—I'm a father myself and I can only imagine what I would do to save my son." Varela nevertheless argues that Salcedo, as depicted in the series, is not a moral man. "He might seem like he's a moral man but that's because he's surrounded by demons. The people he's surrounded by are so fucking vicious that anyone would be looking good if you compare them with the Rodríguez brothers, and you have to be a saint to come across as a decent person. At the end of the day [Salcedo] is not a moral person because a moral person would not work for an organization like this. That

was the most challenging part, making him likeable, approachable but at the same time he's doing immoral things—that was the challenge for me as an actor, how did he do this? How did he create the view of this for the audience to kind of root for this guy even though he's doing all these things in the name of drugs, in the name of violence, in the name of money?"

SALCEDO'S HOUSE

In creating the environment for Jorge Salcedo and his family, Salvador Parra sought to reinforce the idea that Salcedo and his wife and children are constantly under the control of the cartel. Salcedo was an arm of the Cali cartel's obsession with secrecy and security, and the cartel's contrast with the bombastic, public outrages of Escobar called for a very different visual and tonal approach to the third season. The Cali cartel fought to control information: they placed spies throughout Cali's institutions and had control over the city's phone company, and they obsessively wiretapped and bugged members of their own organization, an approach that earned them the nickname "the Cali KGB." Eric Newman often referred to the 2006 German film *The Lives of Others* on the East German Stasi Police while developing the season. Salvador Parra and the show's cinematographers translated these ideas into a claustrophobic, film noir-type atmosphere that set season three apart from the more epic, sunlit scope of the first two seasons.

Parra points out that Salcedo and his family are essentially owned by the Cali cartel from the outset. "His house is a house that you can tell is really rented by the cartel, and his wife that is working as a lawyer—she doesn't know she's working for the cartel but everyone in Cali is working for the cartel. And Salcedo knows about that—he's very clever, he knows what is happening but he cannot leave because he knows he's going to be killed as soon as he gets out." The production designer worked to create a feeling of claustrophobia in order to reflect the idea of Salcedo being trapped. "For me he was a very careful guy in this natural house, this homey home where he was a nice father, but he's starting to get into small places. That's the way he feels at the very end, like he's really trapped and there's no way out, but it's more about his attitude and the way it's written in the episodes: that he's really getting into small spaces. So we thought about ways to squish the guy—like the corridors of his house are too bright for the guy. He's trying very hard to be the perfect father and to have the perfect marriage but he knows that something is wrong so it's the opposite: it's not bright colors, it's dark colors, and he's trying to rescue himself but he's trapped all the time."

"WE THOUGHT ABOUT WAYS TO SQUISH THE GUY"

SALVADOR PARRA

ABOVE AND RIGHT: Final photos of the Salcedo set.

TOP RIGHT: Concept design by Salvador Parra.

PALLOMARI'S OFFICE

Salvador Parra tried to extend his idea of creating a feeling of claustrophobia around Salcedo's character into environments occupied by others, like the business office of cartel accountant Pallomari. "Salcedo is trying to save this character who's in this crazy building that we dressed entirely," Parra said. "It was an abandoned building from the seventies, and we dressed it with all these desks and people like Billy Wilder's *The Apartment*. He's running like a little cockroach inside this very messy building with all these accounting guys working for the cartel. So he's trapped all the time—he's in this little office, he has to try to squeeze inside this little space to try to tap a phone line. He's trying to escape from the cartel which is everywhere and he's just using the little spaces he knows that the Cali cartel don't know about."

ABOVE: Final photos from the set of Pallomari's office.

GUILLERMO PALLOMARI

CHARGED WITH DELIVERING PRODIGIOUS BRIBES to politicians to keep the cartel in business, Pallomari eventually became a marked man, but Salcedo prevented his assassination at the hands of the Cali cartel. Pallomari then became a key element to Salcedo's plan to leave the cartel, and was delivered to the DEA so that he could testify against the cartel. Javier Cámara's droll performance as Pallomari inserts a rare element of humor into the otherwise deadly-suspense vibe of the third season. "He's a brilliant comedic actor in Spain," says producer Carlo Bernard. "He's like the Peter Sellers of Spain, almost a silent movie actor where you don't even understand what he's saying but you understand the character's pomposity and sense of grandiosity. And again, Guillermo Pallomari really existed, he was the cartel accountant who was spirited out of the country and ended up providing a bunch of testimony, so that's based on the truth."

PROFILE:
CHEPE SANTACRUZ LONDOÑO

Running against the grain of the sophisticated, well-heeled Rodríguez brothers, Chepe Londoño, who ran the Cali's New York drug operations, was happily lower class and never hesitated to dirty his hands with the blood of anyone who might interfere with his work for the cartel. Despite being told by Gilberto Rodríguez to keep a low profile in his work in New York City, Chepe (Pêpê Rapazote) managed to jumpstart the third season's action when he cornered members of a Dominican gang that had been using up some of the supply of ether that Chepe needed for his cocaine labs in the city. Cheekily, he made a hair appointment at the salon whose back room the Dominicans operated out of. Chepe then lured the rival gang members into a confrontation and shot them down inside the salon.

"Chepe was a sort of fascinating character and kind of ran the New York operations and seemed to be a sort of larger than life, very colorful, dangerous guy," says executive producer Carlo Bernard. "I think we saw him as a chance to inject some charisma and wildness into the cartel because the Rodríguez brothers and Pacho were relatively low key and a little bit more business-like. Whereas Chepe in real life wore these denim overalls and had this sort of earthy character to him, so that was the part we gravitated toward and tried to play up him as a little bit of a contrast to the Rodríguez brothers being more like bankers in nature." It was Londoño who engineered the relocation of cocaine manufacturing into the U.S., after the DEA made the process too difficult and expensive to pull off in Colombia, by establishing drug labs in the suburbs of New York, Pennsylvania, and Ohio. But after one of his New York labs suffered an explosion and the authorities investigated the murder of a journalist, Londoño had to flee the state.

"WE SAW HIM AS A CHANCE TO INJECT SOME CHARISMA AND WILDNESS INTO THE CARTEL"

CARLO BERNARD

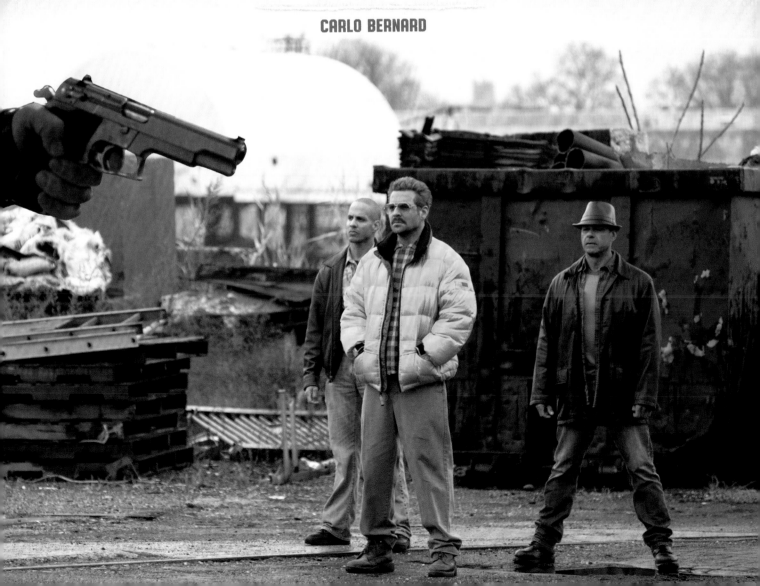

NEW YORK COCAINE LAB

Production designer Salvador Parra applied his prodigious research in cocaine processing and production to design the coke labs run by Chepe in New York City. "We shot a lot in Queens," Parra said. "There was another cocaine lab for Chepe Santacruz in New York that is very sophisticated. He has industrial vans that transport the cocaine and then they have this beautiful room full of crystal cocaine getting dried with electric heaters that give us a different atmosphere, and it looks more like a proper industry. The idea of that set was that these guys from Cali are really smart and they decide if the heater works in Colombia, why don't we make the whole process in New York? That's why in New York it's another set and it's close to the Bronx." Parra also found a luxury apartment for Chepe with an unexpected tie to contemporary politics. "We have a couple of apartments there that we did in one of Trump's buildings—Chepe Santacruz's apartment was a spectacular penthouse with a magnificent view in one of Trump's buildings."

BELOW: Concept design by Salvador Parra.

EXPLODING A DRUG LAB

AFTER HE SLAYED HIS DOMINICAN rivals at the hair salon, Chepe was happy to see the blame for an accidental explosion in one of his labs fall on the Dominicans, which momentarily directed suspicions away from Chepe and his NY operations. But a crusading Cuban journalist who had been scouting out Chepe's activities fingers the Cali cartel and Chepe in his news reports, causing Chepe to track down and murder the reporter. Salvador Parra found the exterior location for the lab in Manhattan, where the explosion effects were rigged outdoors. "All the exteriors of the cocaine labs are in Queens and the interior of the lab that explodes is in a real location. We dressed it as a cocaine lab and we had all the special effects done outside, so that wasn't built."

ARFHOUSE NY

RAID AND CAPTURE

The major twist of season three played out as Gilberto, clearly positioned as the Cali cartel's leader and the antagonist for the Cali story, was captured in a surprise raid and sent to prison. Completely inspired by the real-life events—the foiled ruse with the chicken truck was actually used by the DEA agents to catch the godfather. The capture was a huge shock for viewers because Pablo wasn't brought down till the end of season two but Gilberto was caugt after four episodes.

The details of Gilberto's capture had to be reproduced carefully because the creative team wanted to match the archival footage of the godfather's exit from an airplane after his arrest. Costume designer María Estela Fernández was tasked with matching not only Gilberto's outfit but the clothing worn by the men escorting Gilberto.

The production also shot the capture of Gilberto at one of the houses actually owned by the Cali cartel. "It wasn't one of Gilberto's houses but it was definitely a narco-owned house at some point," says Jesse Rose Moore. "It's just one of those big, crazy houses with so many rooms that you can shoot for days and still not shoot everything."

Production designer Salvador Parra prepped and dressed multiple rooms of the mansion to prepare for the sequence of DEA agents engaging in a painstaking, suspenseful search of the house. The agents eventually discovered Gilberto's *caleta*—a hiding space, in this case constructed under a flight of stairs—the first time the concept of the *caleta* was used in the series.

"IT WAS DEFINITELY A NARCO-OWNED HOUSE AT SOME POINT"

JESSE ROSE MOORE

CALETAS

One of production designer Salvador Parra's most unusual tasks was recreating the ingenious hiding places that the Cali drug lords would have built into their homes, beginning with the location where Gilberto is found in 'Checkmate.' "Gilberto is hiding in a little jacuzzi and that was really funny to make," Parra said. "These guys have a lot of hiding places in their apartments—they would make a little bunker so they would be safe from the police or other cartels. For example, for Miguel, we need this little caleta instead of a bathroom, and you can see that this guy is really trapped in this little hole like a rat, and the DEA guys are inside trying to get him. We designed it so you could see the reactions of both sides, in the bathroom and inside the hole." Parra said that the cartel's hiding places included spaces for equipment and information. "In Miguel's desk he was hiding a little book where he kept all the accounting, so we had to build that—so these guys are hiding information and money and their lives all the time, so it was interesting to design that. Any time you have a narco story you have caletas, some place to hide, and I loved that."

THIS SPREAD: Concept designs and a final photo of the bathroom *caletas*.

ABOVE: Concept sketches of Gilberto in a caleta.

GILBERTO'S TOWN HOUSE

For season three, production designer Salvador Parra looked for locations and a look that would reflect the color of the locale as well as the attitude of the "Gentlemen of Cali." "The Cali cartel, they want to be like regular businessmen, so they don't want to show off like the cartel in Medellín," Parra said. "They try to look like bankers, like the people from society who are invited to all the festivals, that give money and charity to the Cali world. It was just a façade—these guys have a lot of business all around. For me it was the opposite of season two and Pablo Escobar—this was all about offices and beautiful houses, everything shiny, everything clean." Parra took pains in his designs and décor to identify the Cali leaders as distinctively nouveau riche. "The houses should look very luxurious and pretentious, but obviously with the aesthetic of a narco. I don't believe that a guy who was poor in the beginning, and suddenly becomes very rich, necessarily has good taste. All that money doesn't create that—so they're trying to be more sophisticated. For example, Gilberto's house where he gets captured, that's a real location and a house that really belonged to the cartel—it belonged, I think, to Henry Loaiza Ceballos, the Scorpion, and it's owned by another family now."

ABOVE AND RIGHT: Concept designs and a final photo by Salvador Parra.

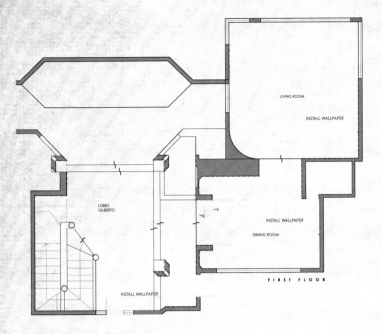

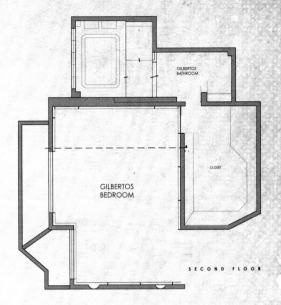

ABOVE: Layout plans for Gilberto's house.

PROFILE:
MIGUEL RODRÍGUEZ

More ruthless than his brother Gilberto, Miguel took increasing control over Cali as Gilberto planned the cartel's exit from the business. Miguel was cut throat but also cautious and never wanted to do any of the "dirty work" himself. He would usually have his more brutal partners take care of any violence—in the first episode he gave Pacho Herrera permission to murder an underling, and then took up with the man's widow. To help make his new lover comfortable, he sent sicarios to retrieve her son from her angry mother-in-law. This infuriated his hotheaded son, David, whose mother Miguel had discarded for the younger woman. After Miguel determined that Salcedo was the rat, he nearly strangled the informant before a DEA raid interrupted him. This act of homicidal fury showed how much Salcedo's betrayal had affected the composed man, who usually never got his hands dirty.

Actor Francisco Denis was cast before much of the third season was planned out—and before the scope of the part of Miguel was realized. "When Francisco was cast in season two he was very much the quiet brother of Gilberto and Damián Alcázar as the big star," Doug Miro says. "What we realized when we got deeper into season three was Gilberto got arrested pretty quickly and ends up having to do a lot of his performing from jail and it's really Miguel's story. And we thought Francisco is great, but can he pull off this much bigger role? There was a lot asked of him in that third season. I don't know if he was anticipating that but he was thrilled to have it and he took it on really well and really ambitiously. It was one of the great gifts of the season for us that he was so good and he was able to do all the things we asked of him."

"They didn't tell me too much about the character at the beginning," Denis says. "They told me who he was and after that I began to read all the books and articles about him. When I came to Bogotá for the first time I took about two weeks to buy all the books to read and to speak with people that had met, not Miguel maybe but people from the cartel." As a native of Venezuela, Denis witnessed a lot of the effects of the Colombian drug war first hand. "For example, I had a friend who was near one of the bombs that went off in Medellín. I met a theater director who was killed—they don't know who exactly but it was by Ochoa or Pablo Escobar or someone else. I knew all these stories because in Venezuela we know all these stories. Everybody was afraid and it was like a war. But like in everything, people get accustomed to it. So it's kind of normal in a way."

Denis was able to listen to vintage recordings of phone conversations between the real Miguel and Gilberto as they planned to bribe a presidential campaign. "This journalist put this cassette out in public so I could hear the voice of Miguel speaking to this guy for three or four hours. So that was the biggest thing I had in my head to work on the character. Miguel was someone who speaks very slowly, and I read a book in which he was described like a man who was really kind of timid, shy—introverted. He didn't like to be with people. But he was very meticulous, very clean—he'd take five showers a day, he would shave himself three times a day, so he was this kind of character, very neat."

For Denis, part of the challenge of the role was creating a convincing relationship both with security expert Jorge Salcedo and Miguel's son David, who in a way would compete for Miguel's trust, putting Miguel in the unusual position of trusting Salcedo over his own son. "I had a conversation with Matias Varela, speaking about Salcedo, and I told Matias it's going to be difficult for the audience to be with your character because you're a traitor. For me Salcedo is the principle character, because he's at the same time a traitor for the Cali cartel, and he's not a good guy. In the show we see that he loves his family, but in real life he was a killer—he was in the middle of this shit, and when he saw he was going to be put in jail also, then he started to think about how to get out. For us, for the Cali characters, he's a traitor, but for the show he's the good guy. When I read the script and every time I talk to the writers, I asked why Miguel is trusting in Salcedo all the time, because he's obviously a traitor."

In his research Denis learned that the real Miguel began to lead the Cali cartel earlier than depicted in the series. "Gilberto went to Madrid to make some contacts and he was living in Madrid in Spain ten years before that, and he was put in jail by the DEA and the police. So at that time Miguel begins to be the leader, and he took Gilberto from the jail in Madrid and brought him back to Bogotá. Gilberto was one year in jail in Bogotá and then he got out. So Miguel is the leader ten years before the show portrays him leading." Denis said that the relationship between Gilberto and Miguel was more like father and son. "For example, when he decides to marry, he asks Gilberto if he can marry this girl and Gilberto says, 'No, you cannot'—and he didn't. In the beginning Gilberto was like his father—he was maybe ten years older, so the older brother was like a father who would tell him what to do and what not to do. Gilberto was really smart—when he was in jail he begins to study philosophy. He's the kind of person who's always thinking on a higher level, but Miguel was very smart in how to share the business."

PROFILE:
DAVID RODRÍGUEZ

Son to Miguel Rodríguez, the second in command in the Cali cartel band of godfathers, David was hotheaded and near psychopathic, a dangerous combination. Although David suspected that Salcedo was the informant who had been undermining the cartel's operations, his father took the side of his security chief, Jorge Salcedo, over his own son. The psychodrama between David Rodríguez, his father Miguel, and Salcedo is one of the dramatic lynchpins of the third season and generates incredible suspense in the season's final episodes. Although according to executive producer Doug Miro, some dramatic license was required to position David Rodríguez as such a dangerous character. "It wasn't clear what David did and didn't do—he did in name only take over the cartel after they all went away [to prison] and was supposedly running it but it was hard to verify that that was true, and we don't really do much with that, it's just a bit in the tenth episode. It's true that Miguel was the guy we characterize him as—he was a quiet, calculating, numbers guy who lived in his brother's shadow but was very smart. You take those facts and extrapolate a little bit but at base there's a lot of truth in those relationships. When David wanted to kill Jorge and Jorge used the tape recorder to record them in the car, that's a true story."

Producer Jesse Rose Moore praised actor Arturo Castro, who's called upon to be more cruel than Miguel Rodríguez's real-life son. "What's incredible is Arturo's on Broad City and he's a comedic actor and he's very funny, and here he's so good. A lot of my friends said, 'I really hated him on the show,' and I thought, 'Well good!' Arturo mostly works in English—he's normally playing American cinema parts and this is his first big dramatic role in Spanish and he did an amazing job."

Executive producer Doug Miro found an element of Shakespeare in the relationships between Miguel, David,

and Salcedo. "The truth of Miguel's story is really fascinating because he had a brother he was trying to eclipse and then there's this parallel story with Salcedo and David, where David is threatened by Salcedo and trying to get his dad's attention."

Actor Francisco Denis says that in playing Miguel, he had to view David as a father would with all the tunnel vision that implies. "Sometimes the reality is right in front of you and you can't accept it. So, David is the only one who knows his father, he doesn't want to push his father to be in the front of the Cartel, and I think they love each other. David loves his father, Miguel loves his son, but Miguel feels his son isn't ready to be the leader and can't trust in him yet."

Denis said he saw the relationship through the lens of his own position as a father. "It's difficult to see our sons like adults. We see them always like a child, and they are not. David, it's a shift of character—he's really cruel, but for me, it's my son, and I want to push him to be the leader but for me he's not ready."

"David is probably the most fictional character in season three," director Andrés Baiz says. "In reality, the Cali cartel wasn't a bloodthirsty cartel and his son wasn't like that. Miguel and Gilberto had a lot of children and I personally know many of them and they are the nicest, most well-educated—zero bullies—so they're not like that at all and David was fictionalized to make the show more entertaining. I'm from Cali so the Cali cartel was always at war with the Medellín cartel and they were always very different. Pablo Escobar was temperamental and used violence to achieve his means, and the Cali cartel was much more like businessmen, low profile, and they didn't like appearing in the press. What they really wanted was for their families to achieve a certain social status and they wanted to quit the business and live normally."

MIGUEL'S ESTATE

Salvador Parra worked to get Miguel Rodríguez's dwelling to reflect the Cali drug lord's fastidious personality. "Gilberto was trying hard to be like a banker and a businessman, and Miguel was more like a guy who will hire an aesthetic decorator—because he was an obsessed guy in every little detail. Like the pool has to be 30 feet long, not 32, not 28, it has to be 30 and you go in and make it right or you get killed." According to Parra, Miguel was modeling his brother Gilberto, but in his own idiosyncratic way. "He's trying to be Gilberto, but we made Gilberto more like a guy trying to have taste and history and convince the world that he's a clean guy who wants to be accepted by society. He's like Michael, like Don Corleone in *The Godfather:* he wants to be in society. But Miguel just wants to be in the business and he understands his brother and the profile of him, but he knows what he's doing. He knows he's been protected by his brother all his life, so now he wants to be himself. So the sets and props we designed for him were for someone who really tries to become someone, but he is lost so he needs help all the time."

"MIGUEL JUST WANTS TO BE IN THE BUSINESS"

SALVADOR PARRA

BELOW: Concept designs by Salvador Parra.

ABOVE: A meeting with the Cali cartel.

SHOOTING IN DIFFERENT SETTINGS

ABOVE: Director Josef Kubota Wladyka on set.

ABOVE: Directors Fernando Coimbra (top) and Andrés Baiz (bottom) watch over scenes.

Cinematographer Luis David Sansans strove to create a contrast between the gritty atmosphere of Bogotá and Cali's tropical environs. "I put some gold fill light for the Cali guys for the idea of their environment. Medellín was all about mountains and heights of the locations. The people in Cali were more tropical—it was the capital of salsa music. The colors were different and the traditions were different which was something you could use to play with the atmosphere of every shoot." Sansans also chose different lenses than the ones used to shoot the first two seasons of the show. "The lenses are sharper than the lenses we used for

Escobar because the cinematographer for season one decided to use vintage lenses to recreate that historical look, because Pablo was from the 80s. The moment we have in season three was more in the 90s, so I chose lenses that were a little more modern than the others, so that creates another texture. We also used less handheld—there was a transition between handheld and more static shots or dolly shots or Steadicam shots by design because of the complexity of the Cali cartel. They were not that violent, so we didn't need to move the camera the way we did with Escobar which was more visceral."

PROFILE: FRANKLIN AND CHRISTINA JURADO

Flashy, sports car driving money launderer to the Cali cartel, Franklin Jurado (Miguel Ángel Silvestre) lived a lavish, globetrotting lifestyle as he laundered cash all over the world. Along with Guillermo Pallomari, Franklin organized the cartel's web of money laundering, shady business deals, bribes, and expenses. The Harvard-educated Jurado met his wife Christina (Kerry Bishé) in college and the two moved to Colombia when Franklin became involved with the Cali cartel.

In a series dedicated to the history of the cocaine trade, Christina Jurado is notable as the first major character shown to be actively using cocaine. And, dramatically, this works to reinforce the idea that, despite the genteel demeanor of the Gentlemen of Cali and their determination to be seen as businessmen, they were still drug dealers.

Despite Peña's best efforts, Christina resisted his charms as he attempted to ingratiate himself with her to get closer to her husband. This was a huge failure for Peña in cultivating and protecting an informant as Franklin was assassinated in prison and Christina was kidnapped on behalf of the Cali cartel—necessitating a daring jungle raid by Peña and military commandos to rescue her. These events raised the stakes for Jorge Salcedo, as it demonstrated that his trust in the DEA may not be rewarded. The raid on the FARC compound was one of several important *Narcos* scenes shot in the jungles of Colombia. This jungle scene was shot a couple of hours outside of Bogotá. "Kerry [Bishé] was such a good sport about it," says producer Jesse Rose Moore. "She was actually very excited to be shooting in the jungle and be out in the middle of nowhere. Her other show was *Halt and Catch Fire*, about computer programmers so it was a huge difference for her going from that to this."

NORTH VALLEY ATTACK

One of the unintended consequences of Miguel and Gilberto Rodríguez's announced plan to surrender to the authorities was the opposition with the North Valley cartel. At the time, the North Valley cartel were part of the Cali operation and they were offended that their opinions hadn't been taken into consideration. While Gilberto and the godfathers had already amassed their fortunes and were ready to "resign", the North Valley cartel hadn't and had no interest in leaving the drug trade. After the arrest of Gilberto, the North Valley cartel members saw the resulting power vacuum as an opportunity to take over the organization.

Two simultaneous assaults by the North Valley cartel on a nightclub party and Pacho's estate started the violent run of the season. The event was a big dramatic turning point for the character of Miguel who surprised everyone with how coldly he enforced his new role as cartel leader in the aftermath.

The integral party scene was filmed in a real nightclub on location in Cali, and was interspersed with shots from the attack on Pacho's estate. This technique, plus the smoke machine and music from the club, helped to add to the chaotic atmosphere of the sequence.

BELOW: Concept design by Salvador Parra.

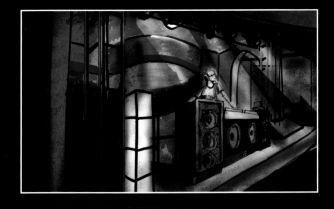

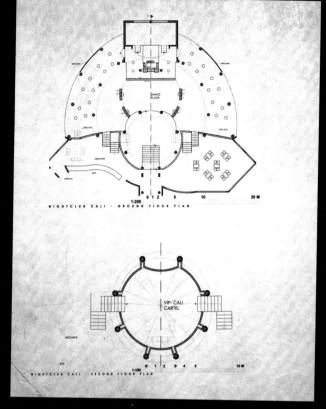

ABOVE: Feistl and Van Ness chase the attackers through the club.

ABOVE: Layout plans for the club where one of the attacks occured.

PROFILE:
PACHO HERRERA

Another stylish playboy, Pacho Herrera (Alberto Ammann) worked in New York, where he funneled drugs into the New York party scene and eventually ran afoul of the Medellín cartel. He proved himself entirely unafraid to confront and irritate Pablo Escobar and his men while he negotiated secretly with the Ochoa brothers as a violent territorial war erupted between the Medellín and Cali cartels. Perfectly comfortable with the brutal tactics of cartel warfare, Pacho's daring included kidnapping and attempting to blackmail DEA Agent Murphy; siding with widow Judy Moncada and the Rodríguez brothers against Escobar; and undercutting Escobar's Miami operations with Cali's foothold there. Pacho also personally initiated the assassination of a rival, Claudio Salazar, outside a club by tying the man between two motorcycles and tearing his body into pieces. This momentous scene was a favorite of Andrés Baiz, "Season three was the most personal for me," Baiz says. "One of the scenes in *Narcos* I'm most proud of is the Pacho dance, the scene where he kisses his boyfriend and then kills [Salazar]. I'm a big salsa fan and

"PACHO IS SO ESSENTIALLY FORMIDABLE THAT HIS PARTNERS ACCEPT HIM"

CARLO BERNARD

that was a scene I got to design every single detail—choosing the extras, the song, the location, so season three has a special resonance to me."

After escaping an assassination attempt by a rival cartel, North Valley, Pacho launched a raid on the ranch of Gerda Salazar, he killed Salazar and then surrendered to police, only to be shot down in prison by a rival sicario.

Producer Carlo Bernard notes that Pacho's volatility and his sexuality never threatened his standing or the stability of the Cali cartel. "The Rodríguez brothers are brothers and the other two partners are Chepe Santacruz and Pacho, and by all accounts these guys didn't ever really turn on each other. We certainly play the conflicts between them in season three but for the most part it was a remarkable partnership. Pacho was younger than the other three guys and he was openly gay and

they all accepted and worked with him, which seems pretty cool and interesting from our point of view; it was a remarkable thing. In the show Pacho is the cruel one—he's the youngest and he was the one that was the cool one, but the godfathers had a pretty successful partnership which is unusual." Given the customary, machismo ethic of the drug lords, Pacho's sexuality is rarely, if ever, mentioned or used as a weapon against Herrera. "We took the point on the show that Pacho is so essentially formidable that his partners accept him, because they're friends with him and they know how good he is at what he does. Other people who might not accept him basically keep their mouths shut because they know what's good for them," says Bernard. "That Pacho can exist as a gay man in that world because he is so hard and so powerful and formidable is an interesting dynamic to play, certainly in that culture in the 90s."

ABOVE: Pacho was the first member of the Cali cartel introduced on *Narcos*—he was brought into the show in season one.

ABOVE: Surveying the bodies, Pacho shows his ruthless colors.

INSIDE THE WALLS

One of the most suspenseful sequences in the entire series involved Miguel Rodríguez disappearing inside one of his houses after it was invaded by DEA officers who were sent to arrest him. Failing to find the drug lord but certain he hadn't escaped the premises, some of the DEA men measured the inside of the house and determined that the internal measurements indicated the presence of a hidden space behind one of the walls where Miguel may be hiding. In an agonizing scene, one of the agents used a massive, 1" diameter drill to poke through parts of the wall, gradually striking nearer and nearer a terrified Miguel and even grazing his arm. Producer Doug Miro says the scene was based on fact. "The drill bit, whether it actually nicked him nobody knows if that's true, but he was inside a wall breathing from an oxygen tank. Big portions of it are true—a lot of the big events, a lot of the events you see and think are crazy—things like the scene of him in the wall, we don't have archival footage of that, we just have peoples' word."

Actor Francisco Denis says that shooting the scene was almost as frightening as what the real-life Miguel went through. "We shot that twice, because the drill was not close enough to me, so when you saw it through the camera at the beginning we thought it was okay and we can believe in that, but when the editors saw that they said 'No, you have to shoot that again because the drill looks too far from him.' So the second time, the drill was really, really near my head, and I was really scared. It was a terrible experience. (I'm claustrophobic) and even if you know there's no problem and everything is secure, just to be there, because it's a real drill and real walls and I'm trapped between two walls, so when you see that scene I wasn't acting."

LEFT: Concept of Miguel hiding inside the walls.

A LEAK IS DISCOVERED

n the climax of the Salcedo storyline, Miguel finally connected the dots and came close to having Salcedo asphyxiated just before the DEA agents moved in to capture him.

"It's always tricky when you're doing a stunt with an actor like that," producer Jesse Rose Moore said of the asphyxiation scene played by Francisco Denis and Matias Varela. "Obviously your first concern is, 'He has a plastic bag over his head and how many times is he going to be okay doing this?' I think the chair fell over backwards and there's inherent, not risk, but you want to make sure that safety is the top priority but that it also looks real. Matias was a very good sport about that and it was a very intense moment in the show when you realize Miguel knows that Salcedo had sold them out." Moore said that the actors sold this intense scene well, including Arturo Castro as David Rodríguez. "Poor David—he's been saying the entire show, 'don't listen to [Salcedo]' and finally his father listens. It's a testament to the actors and to the story that people really latched on to the third season and loved it. It's a very tense season, more of a thriller than the previous season and it had such a broad cast of characters."

Flushed from his apartment while in the act of trying to kill Salcedo, Miguel fled in his car only to be blocked by DEA agents in a van, leading the injured godfather to crawl from his wrecked car and surrender to the authorities.

Cinematographer Luis David Sansans worked to add to the claustrophobic tension of season three's suspenseful Jorge Salcedo plotline. "It was more about spy games. It was another kind of violence—psychological violence with the character of Salcedo. He has to forget about his plans in life to be dedicated to his family and abandon the cartel, and he doesn't know how to handle that situation, and he starts to get in a conflict with himself about how to get out, and every time he finds a solution there's a new situation that's worse than the last one. He has to stay and at some point the only choice he has is to try to get [his Cali employers] in jail and to betray his bosses and work with the DEA. That becomes a double game which is extremely dangerous for his family, for himself and for his friends and the people he loves." Sansans said that the third season's focus on character and tension presented a switch from the epic carnage of the Pablo Escobar story. "That was a challenge too because there was not a lot of chase sequences and action sequences, it was more introverted with the characters and their feelings, and that's why we decided to make it a little more aesthetic and create tension with slow pushes and telephoto lenses and be more with the actors. I think that was the change and the narrative we chose for season three. There were no shootouts or things like that: my job was to maintain the tension through the season in a different way."

ABOVE: Salcedo and Miguel in calm conversation before the confrontation.

VIOLENT SURRENDER

s the third season reached its conclusion, the series centered one of its most stylish action sequences on the popular character of Pacho Herrera. With Gilberto and Miguel under arrest and Pacho's brother Alvero crippled by a North Valley raid, Pacho launched a final attack on the North Valley leaders. Pacho was seeking out the aging Gerda Salazar, the embittered mother of Miguel's mistress and author of the attack on Alvero Herrera as well as failed attempts at Pacho's life. Well-known Colombian actress Vicky Hernández, who played Gerda, is actually the mother of actor Juan Sebastián Calero, who played Navegante.

The sequence highlighted the way Pacho placed his own personal vendettas ahead of his responsibilities to the cartel,

as well as the character's ingeniously savage methods of carrying out revenge. In this case he used two armed, attractive young women on motorcycles to distract and take out the North Valley guards on the highway before Pacho himself entered the cartel leaders' compound to wreak havoc.

The opening scenes of the assault were shot in part of the region's North Valley, with trees covered in a haze of spider webs adding a surreal frame for the motorcycle action. Having Pacho stride through a tracking shot of choreographed mayhem inside the North Valley estate compound reinforced the character's suave, indestructible demeanor, while touches of black comedy (including a fleeing, nude woman) added to the chaos of the moment.

ABOVE: Pacho leads an attack on the North Valley cartel.

PROFILE:
JORGE "EL NAVEGANTE" VELASQUEZ

One of the Cali cartel's most trusted *sicarios*, Navegante (Juan Sebastián Calero) penetrated the Medellín cartel at the beginning of the turf war between the Cali cartel and the Medellín cartel and gave information leading to the DEA's capture of José Rodríguez Gacha. He became an important bodyguard to Cali godfathers Gilberto and Miguel Rodríguez and Pacho Herrera, working with Herrera in Miami. Navegante was ordered to abduct Jorge Salcedo after the Cali cartel discovered that he was the informant but refrained from killing Salcedo, who he liked, knowing that David Rodríguez would happily do the job. A desperate Salcedo took advantage of Navegante's hesitation so that he could save his own life.

"We cast him in season one," producer Jesse Rose Moore says of Navegante. "He was supposedly working for Gacha but then later you find out he's actually working for Cali and he's sold out Gacha. He acts as if he was an informant to Peña, but really he's selling out Gacha on behalf of Cali." Moore credits the *Narcos*' creative team and their enjoyment of actor Juan Sebastián Calero's work in the role for expanding Navegante's profile in the series. "Juan Sebastián Calero is a great actor—he'd auditioned for us and he's someone Andrés Baiz really liked and wanted to find a role for. He seemed perfect for [Navegante] and Eric and Chris agreed and everyone thought he was great, and then he became a character that stuck around for all three seasons in Colombia. Juan Sebastián really created things very subtly—he never was over the top, he was always just sort of present in a scene and then he'd do something that was really interesting."

SALCEDO AND THE SICARIO

SEEMINGLY OUT OF THE WOODS after the arrest of Miguel Rodríguez, Jorge Salcedo found himself tasked with bringing in the Cali's accountant Pallomari, which led to a confrontation with the *sicario* Navegante, who had been assigned to kill Pallomari. Faced with a fateful choice, Salcedo grabbed Navegante's pistol and shot the hitman the only outright murder Salcedo committed in the line of duty. "That relationship was so interesting because they were so different," actor Matias Varela says of the dynamic between Salcedo and Navegante "At the same time they kind of like each other, and then Salcedo ends up killing him. That's the only person he kills through the entire show, the only time he fires a gun. And he fires a gun at the guy who says, 'Why do you hate guns?'"

NAVEGANTE'S PERSONAL BELONGINGS

NAVEGANTE'S PROPS INDICATE THE LIFESTYLE of a hired killer: a baroque torture instrument in the form of elaborate brass knuckles, two different switchblade knives, a gold crucifix necklace and a keychain replete with Catholic religious bling, and a wallet sewn with two skull images.

THE END OF THE GENTLEMEN OF CALI

The Colombian police and the U.S. DEA had managed to imprison the Cali godfathers, and they could safely bring their sources into custody. The testimonies in court uncovered the cartel's influence over the government and caused a political backlash between Colombia and the U.S. Peña discovered that the Cali godfathers were going to get an easy ride; they had donated to the president's campaign in exchange for virtual immunity. His disappointment in bureaucracy forced him to act out and, knowingly putting his job at risk, he released tapes that revealed the corruption in the highest levels of the government. Forced by pressure from the public and press to act, Colombia and the U.S. reinstated Escobar's most-feared punishment: extradition.

The Cali cartel came to an ignominious end when Miguel and Gilberto Rodríguez were transported to new prisons within the U.S. Then the North Valley cartel leader Orlando Henao Montoya, after surviving Pacho's attack on the North Valley compound, decided to take his vengeance. David Rodríguez was gunned down in the street just as the ambitious son of Miguel Rodríguez was about to take up the reins of the Cali cartel while the rest of its leaders were imprisoned. Montoya's retribution for the attack on the North Valley cartel headquarters was completed when he arranged for sicarios to murder Pacho Herrerra in jail. And finally, Chepe Santacruz was killed by members of the AUC paramilitary group, bringing an end to the Gentlemen of Cali—and season three.

Ending the Colombia story with the same dynamic aesthetic as it had started, director Andrés Baiz created a masterful blend of series and documentary footage. The last episode featured real-life newscasts, press conferences from President Samper, footage of President Clinton, and the riots in Bogota.

The creators of the show aimed to match the death scenes as closely as possible and the final three deaths played out as a blend of fact and fiction. The restaurant location where David was shot had actually been established as a Cali hangout in the show's first season. Pacho Herrera frequented the restaurant in season one, then Miguel in season three, and finally David Rodríguez conducted business at the restaurant established as a meeting place for his father—so in effect the restaurant location helped illustrate the rise and ultimate fall of the Cali cartel.

While there were no photos of the actual Pacho's death in prison, the production matched the circumstances of Herrera's end as closely as possible. Better-documented was the death of Chepe Santacruz, and photographs of this circumstance (aired in the episode) allowed Chepe's clothing and even the actual position of the bullet wounds on his body to be matched to the way his death played out historically.

The third season finale wrapped up the Colombian drug cartel story, weaving the narratives of the four Cali godfathers as well as agent Peña, Jorge Salcedo and the fallout from Peña's alliances within the cartels and its impact on volatile U.S.-Colombian relations, all into a dramatically satisfying and historically resonant coda. With Peña resigning his post and returning home to Texas, the last few scenes of the season gave an idea of the next target: a conversation between Mike Spencer and Javier Peña over Kiki Camarena and a comment from Peña's father undoubtedly leads towards Mexico.

ABOVE RIGHT: Chepe, Pacho, and David were violently removed as heads of the cartel.

GUADALAJARA

In season four, *Narcos* turns to Mexico and the Guadalajara cartel. We told Colombia's story through the Cali cartel, and after that Colombia disintegrates into a bunch of smaller warring factions," producer Doug Miro says.

"The North Valley cartel is interesting and you see a little of them in season three but there wasn't enough of them to do a season. So Eric's idea really was to go to Mexico and cover the Mexican drug trade with the interest of getting up to today, but we wanted to start with what is the most famous DEA Mexican drug story which is Kiki Camarena. It's the same structural idea—the DEA story is Kiki and Kiki is going after the very first Mexican drug cartel which is called the Guadalajara cartel." Formed by Miguel Ángel "Félix" Gallardo, who came to Guadalajara and formed a cartel using contacts from his native Sinaloa to move marijuana across the U.S. border via the various plazas or territories—then converted that system for cocaine.

ZACATECAS RANCH

ABOVE: Concept art of the season four location.

Gallardo becomes the central narco figure of season four: a kind of tragic hero, a visionary ultimately undone by his own megalomania. "It starts in 1980 and moves all the way to 1985 and it tracks, on Félix's side, the rise of his marijuana empire then his cocaine empire, and on Kiki's side his pursuit of Félix," Miro says of the story. "It's at a stage when the DEA was very early days and they were still very much at the point of confiscating as much drugs as possible, delivering intelligence from the south in Mexico to the border in the U.S. so they could seize drugs when they came over the border. They're much less interested at that point in time in going after the guys behind these cartels, but Kiki and his guys in Guadalajara were one of the first groups to say let's go after the guys behind the cartel, and they went after Félix, and the story of them going after Félix and the way their stories are entangled becomes this sort of epic tragedy at the end of the season for both of them, and sets in motion the following years of the Mexican drug wars."

As the show has expanded and evolved from Pablo Escobar to the Colombian drug cartels and into Mexico and beyond, it has consistently surprised with its range and scope—but creator Eric Newman says the intent has always been to tell a broader story. "Our show was never about Pablo Escobar, it wasn't about the Cali cartel, it was about cocaine—this incredibly volatile, dangerous, desirable thing that just continues on because it's never the thing we're ever trying to address. We're attacking the plants that yield it or the people who sell it to us and what we never address is that we're the largest market for cocaine in the world by far and somehow in a uniquely American way we're unable to look inward. We're much better at finding an antagonist or an enemy out there where we can say that's the problem, there's some brown guy in Colombia, or Ecuador, or wherever that keeps sending us this shit that we don't want."

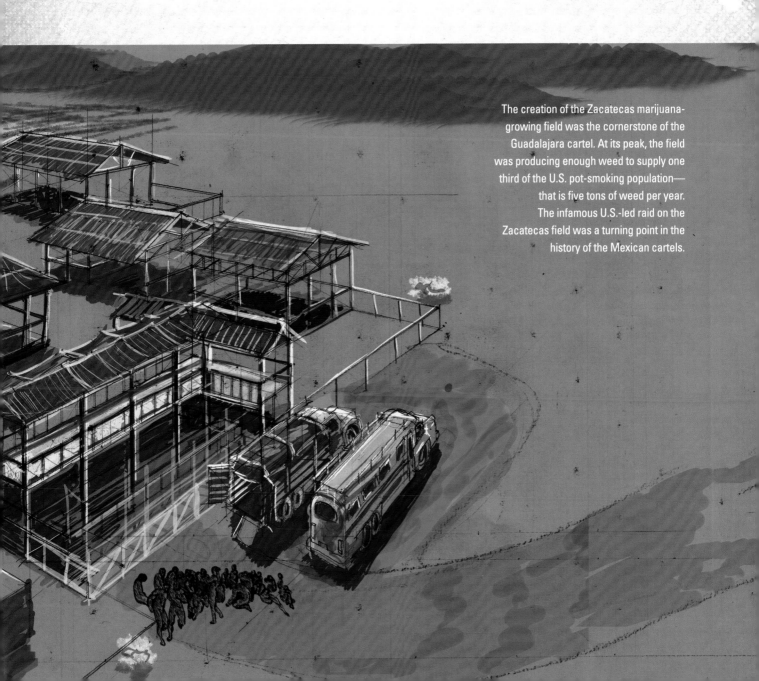

The creation of the Zacatecas marijuana-growing field was the cornerstone of the Guadalajara cartel. At its peak, the field was producing enough weed to supply one third of the U.S. pot-smoking population—that is five tons of weed per year. The infamous U.S.-led raid on the Zacatecas field was a turning point in the history of the Mexican cartels.

ACKNOWLEDGEMENTS

Thanks to all of the brilliant creative personnel behind Narcos who gave so generously of their time to provide input for this book including Eric Newman, Chris Brancato, Doug Miro, Carlo Bernard, Andrés Baiz, Jesse Rose Moore, Wagner Moura, Francisco Denis, Matias Varela, Luis David Sansans, Salvador Parra, and Alexandra Hunter. And thanks to everyone who assisted me in tracking them down including Ali Sabbah, Travis Rutherford, Kirsti Tichenor, Tim Stephen, Danielle Bicer, Jackson Kellard, Brent Travers, Julian Savodivker, Peter Micelli, Brandon Finkelstein, Rob Kenneally, Tiffany Ward, Susan H. Bodine, Paul Hook, Ryan Gilbert, Carlos Carreras, Stephanie Simon, Jacob Hernandez, Cherie Johnson, Katrina Bayonas, Kimberly Jaime, and Brandon Alinger at The Prop Store for the beautiful photos of the props.

DEDICATION

To my father, Kenneth Bond, who went from being an alcoholic shoe salesman to an alcohol and drug counselor and eventually was appointed by the governor of Ohio to the Council on Alcohol and Drug Addiction Services. He ran the alcohol and drug recovery program for four counties in Northwest Ohio for many years. Still the greatest success story I can think of.

OCEAN

Clipperton I. France

Darwin I.

Galapagos Is. Ecuador

Isabela I.

Hatutu I.
Un Huka I.
Hiva Oa I.
Mohotani I.

MARQUESAS ISLAND
France

Napuka I.
Pukapuka I.

ARCHPELAGO ISLANDS

Fangatau I.
Raroia I.
Hao I.
Tatakoto I.

Vanavana I.

Marutea I. New Zealand

Marokau I.
Tematangi I.
Morane I.
Gambier I.

Maratiri I.

Henderson I. U.K.
Pitcairn I. U.K.

Easter I. Chile

SOUTH PACIFIC OCEAN

PACIFIC OCEAN